140 Photography Puzzles

Word Searches
Word Scrambles
Cryptograms

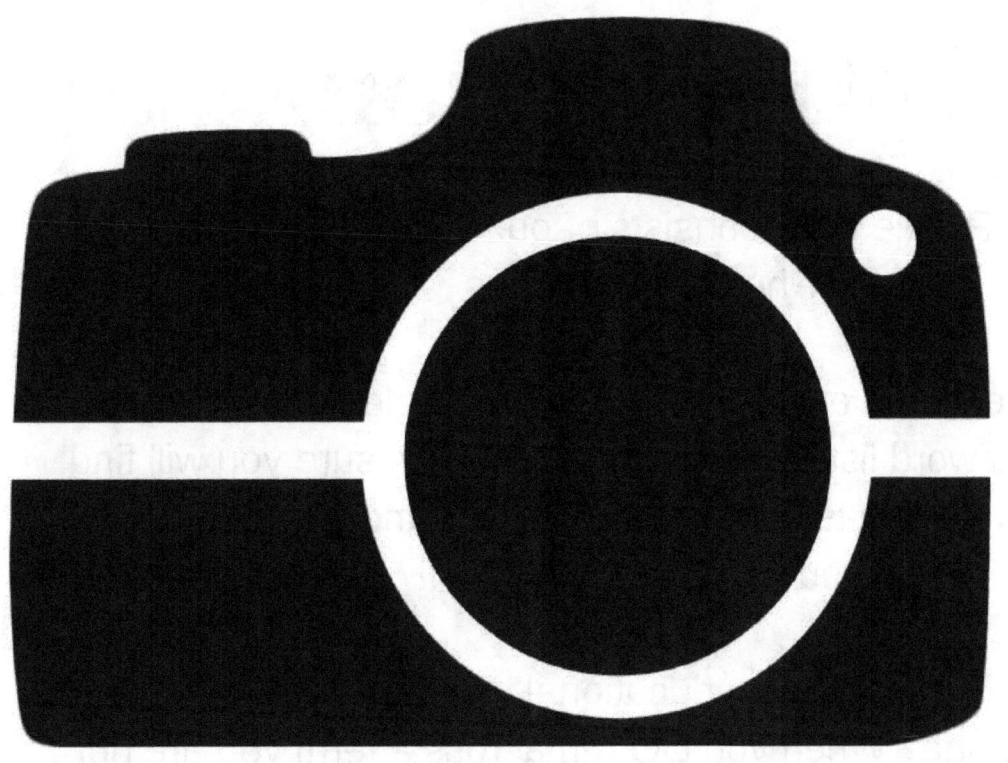

This Puzzle Book
Belongs To:

_____

Introduction

This Puzzle book consists of puzzles made up of PhotographyTerms

Many of the words are used in multiple puzzles - but in total, I drew from a word list of about 800 words. I'm sure you will find almost every photo term you can think of, and hundreds more you've NEVER heard of!

Want to turn this into an educational tool as well as have an extra challenge? When you DO run across a term you are not familiar with... Try to guess at its' meaning, then look it up to see if you were right!

I designed these puzzles to be tough - but solvable! You are going to have a lot of fun working out the solutions.
PLUS -
I guarantee that... You will learn some new photo terms AND you'll get a lot of insight and inspiration from the quotes!!

This book is going to provide you with hours and hours of FUN!

Word Searches

Photography #1

```
T H N E Y U E P K S M E T E R W L R A G L
B U L B C N T S R P E X U R I N S E T N W
L U M E N E A M M E R Z E Q B F L A G I B
L E S A E M T E A C S J I V A E M R P R P
N W D D R M O O Z T Y E E S O P A E O P O
L A E E A A R W A R C R R S T C O M T E P
R R P K P G X Y I U D U O V N N H A S T E
P M U A S F E N D M L I T M A E I C P S N
I C O H N A T M E B O H F T E T L R T T U
T O L S A M T T M S U C O F E M I R P A M
C L Y A R R A S C R E E N U U R I V V N B
H O M K T D M N R R E S I N V S P E E D R
R R A D A P T E R R E D E Y E F E Y F H A
O S F T F P L E S A A S S Z U Q I A C A D
M H A R I L N M C M Y H I J K M Y L O Z I
A I A X I N N O I T A Z I R A L O P T E R
K M E H A I G S T R O B E G D G I S O E G
E L O C C I G A P I C L E D O M O S F R R
Y Y S A T R N N O P U S L B K H C R O P P
A G D Z I D G Y H O O D O I G M A T R I X
T H O P X Z R O M D F F T R F C L I P U P
```

Photography Word List #1

Adapter

Agfa

Array

Batch

Beam

Blur

Bulb

Camera

Chromakey

Coating

Cove

Crop

Diffuse

Easel

Fill

Flag

Frame

Fuji

Gel

Ghost

Gitzo

Gobo

Grid

Grip

Haze

Hood

Hoya

Hurrell

Image

Kit

Kodak

Loupe

Lumen

Man Ray

Mask

Mat cutter

Matrix

Matte

Media

Memory

Menu

Metadata

Meter

Model

Nadar

NiCad

Opaque

Optics

Pan

Penumbra

Pitch

Pixel

Play

Polarization

Pop

Pose

Preservative

Prime focus

Print sizes

Profoto

Prop

Pupil

Raw

Red eye

Resin

Rinse

Riser

Rotate

Sanyo

Scanner

Screen

Scrim

Set

Shake

Sharp

Shim

Silk

Skew

Spectrum

Speed

Stand

Step ring

Stop

Strobe

Transparency

Tripod

UV filter

VR lens

Warm colors

Zoom

Photography #2

```
P O R P O P D M M E N U A T E E D A H S L
F O A F I N E A R T Z L Y N K R E S I N E
B E R E R I F T M E B A O I V A A F L A G
L E L C T C O T M U M T H R O L Y M P U S
U H I U S A C E M S D O I P F F G I T Z O
R E P R O D U C T I O N T L B S T H V O O
R Y U N H J S E M W A I L E N A G S B P G
E E P O G O P Z F M C I K E L I G O S F L
T C L K B R E I S S F I L L L I G H T U A
T U A I I M N L M P O S E Y S L O W L J S
U P Y N A F A A T A M R A C A O G L W I S
H L G R I H T U H E B D A T T D E E L B E
S C F N E B Y S V M S L I R Y I B K U G S
A M I W O E R I U M E G C R C R G L A P K
N T O A H L T V F P I R G A G H B M E H J
Y M R O S L E E O D I R I S N O I E A N S
O D E T Z O M R H K C T R I P O D V A S D
X J O D P W M P N O O W C O C D N E E M K
A P L A O S Y K I D V A X H R T N A D A R
M I N O X M S I L A E R O T O H P O I N T
C O N T R A S T J K S N O R A A M I L S V
```

Photography Word List #2

Album

Archive

Beam

Bellows

Bleed

Blend

Blur

Bulb

Canon

Contrast

Cove

Crop

Daylight

Defocus

Digital

Eye cup

Fill flash

Fill light

Fine art

Fire

Flag

Flare

Frame

Fuji

Gel

Ghost

Gitzo

Glass

Gobo

Grid

Grip

Halsman

Haze

Hood

Hoya

Image

Infinity

Iris

Joule

Kit

Kodak

Leica

Lens

Linhof

Mask

Matboard

Matte

Menu

Midtone

Minox

Mirror

Modem

Mosaic

Nadar

NiCad

Nikon

Olympus

Optics

Pan

Photorealism

Pitch

Play

Point

Pop

Pose

Previsualize

Print

Prop

Pupil

Raw

Remote

Reproduction

Resin

Sanyo

Scale

Set

Shade

Shake

Shim

Shoe

Shoot

Shutter

Silk

Slim Aarons

Speed

Step ring

Stop

Symmetry

Tamrac

Tripod

Umbrella

Zoom

Photography #3

```
N A D A R R E W I N D F I L T E R P W K J
E L A C I R T E M M Y S A U R S U C O F L
P R I N T B O K E H A Z E I E P E N Y E L
E O H S Y Y E S H A R P S V I R I O D Z I
Y B T P A P E R S A F E Y L O C E K D I F
E J P F U N I K K O R T T R A C K I U L H
D E G O U J G H W X H N I E P C E N M A S
E C L R R J R E M O T E C D M M O D E U A
R T A E A P I K I T L C A M N E M U L S L
M L N L G I P T R A N S P A R E N C Y I F
E E D I B A N A L O G E O T N B L U R V V
G N S S O U V B E A M D D I R G Y B L E S
A S C C N P M E D E E N E U J A G F A R P
P C A I G A L F R I D A R T L E U Q A P O
I R P T S I P A O N I C Y P E A S E L P T
X I E P F I R E C W A N D O B N M I H S L
E M C O R A L U C O A I S M H B T K R N I
L C R O P E I K N R F R E S L E I C A I G
U P R O O F S Q Y B A T T E R Y P A C K H
O S T U D I O I S V S O E S O P S N O O T
J P O W E R U P N W P D I G I T A L Q C O
```

Photography Word List #3

Agfa

Album

Analog

Asymmetrical

Battery pack

Beam

Bleed

Blend

Blur

Bokeh

Brownie

Cokin

Cove

Crop

Detent

Digital

Easel

Fire

Flag

Flash fill

Focal point

Focus

Fuji

Gel

Grain

Grid

Grip

Haze

Hoya

Incandescent

Iris

Joule

Kit

Konica

Landscape

Leica

Loupe

Low key

Lumen

Lumiere

Mat

Media

Megapixel

Menu

Meter

Mode

Muddy

Nadar

ND Filter

Niepce

Nikkor

Nikon

Object lens

Ocular

Opacity

Opaque

Optics

Pan

Paper safe

Play

Pose

Power up

Previsualize

Print

Profile

Proof

Prop

Pupil

Raw

Red eye pen

Remote

Resin

Rewind

Riser

Scrim

Set

Sharp

Shim

Shoe

Silk

Skew

Snoot

Spotlight

Stop

Studio

Sync cord

Track

Transparency

Photography #4

```
C U R T A I N N O I S N E T X E N B P W R
P R A S Y M M E T R I C A L I Y D O G E N
O E V I H C R A P K O D A K X V R A I K O
T A M R A C U A O V P L A N E C P R H S N
S I R E S I N C E C N A L L I E V R U S E
F D K H S A L F M O O Z L Y A Y O H I L X
P E I A J V I L U M I N E S C E N C E S B
O M A Z L L E X I P Z M S J L C C I W E M
R D N E L B X K A G E R A L G U A L A O S
T D I V T O P S T O H Y E M E P M M I N H
R C T E B A T C H X S T E B I G E E E C S
A D E O O E R I N S E N S O R Y R L N I K
I O R G L H L E O P U P C O N T A X X S M
T P S O N A S L S I R I A M U G M A T T E
P I T B M I G O O I R T L E X R F T E S T
L R U O L J N F Z W R C E F P F C T G N E
A T D K M E G R A T S H I X O O C E A O R
Y E I I I Q E A U Q I S M W A R P A T O I
M F O O R P Q D L B G G A W R M D R N T N
E S O P C G I J U F M W G L M A S K O O G
F I R E S A E L E R A E E D G T T I M P N
```

Photography Word List #4

Agfa

Archive

Asymmetrical

Batch

Beam

Bellows

Bleed

Blend

Blurry

Boom

Burning

Canon

Click

Cokin

Contax

Cove

Crop

Curtain

Easel

Extension

Eye cup

F stop

Fill

Fire

Flag

Format

Fuji

Gel

Gitzo

Glare

Glass

Glossy

Gobo

Grid

Haze

Hot spot

Hoya

Ilford

Image

Iris

Kit

Kodak

Leica

Lens

Light source

Lumen

Luminescence

Mamiya

Mask

Matte

Media

Menu

Metering

Modem

Montage

Noise

Off axis

On camera

Pan

Pastel

Pitch

Pixel

Plane

Play

Pop

Portrait

Pose

Prism

Proof

Prop

Raw

Release

Resin

Retina

Rinse

Riser

Scale

Scrim

Sensor

Set

Shade

Shim

Shoe

Sigma

Silk

Skew

Snoot

Studio

Surveillance

Tamrac

Tripod

Xenon

Zoom flash

Photography #5

```
R A D A N T N I R P R E V I S U A L I Z E
O A G F A I L T D T P E H J P O K S E W R
T E P H P K A O H U Z B A U U E M L Z M A
C R O P O M C G O A O Q T F M U S L I N W
E I R I S S I L H O U E T T I N G I R S F
J F P E T L T H M E S T R E E T P H O T O
O V E R E X P O S U R E I G L G O E L N R
R M O F E N O P A Q U E C N B R V K O O M
P B A N R I O D U O B S K I A I E O C O A
E S O S E T T I N G S H O T T D R B D F T
F N W M K Y Y O T I A A D A T S L E L P T
S N E L L A C O F A W D A O H P I A R O E
S N S A L E I C A S Z E K C G O G L A S S
U L T P O T S F K Y H I R D I T H R E E L
O B O G N B E A M F L A R E L N T N I G I
T Q N I S Y B Z O B L U R A O I N I M P N
P L A N E F M F U K B I P P L K I K A E H
D R O C I V L E N A S I E P Z O O O G O O
G O U L B A O V T E X N O O X N P C E H F
T P L E S A E C R E U P O K K F O C U S F
A Y O H O M H O L P R M N R E T T U H S Z
```

Photography Word List #5

Afocal lens

Agfa

Batch

Beam

Blur

Bokeh

Boom

Boudoir

Coating

Cokin

Colorize

Cove

Crop

Easel

Eye cup

F stop

Fill

Fire

Flag

Flare

Flash

Focus

Fuji

Gel

Ghost

Glass

Gobo

Grain

Gridspot

Grip

Hat trick

Haze

Hoya

Image

Iris

Kit

Kodak

Leica

Light table

Linhof

Loupe

Mask

Matte

Menu

Meter

Mode

Mount

Muslin

Nadar

Nikon

Noise

Opaque

Open up

Optical

Overexposure

Overlight

Pan

Pixel

Plane

Play

Point

Polarization

Pop

Pose

Previsualize

Print

Projector

Prop

Raw format

Rewind

Riser

Safelight

Settings

Setup

Shade

Sharp

Shim

Shoe

Shutter

Silhouetting

Silk

Snoot

Street photo

Strobe

Weston

Xenon

Zoom

Photography #6

```
R W M A G N I F Y I N G S P P N O H T K U
K T N W O L D M X G R H P K O P B M C P E
D P R O F O T O U A O C G T T R A C E U H
P C F O B E I U N E M O S I E E C N L K O
D I R G V N O N A C L E C G B C K R F C T
S D S O M F Y T W A W A A F O A D E E A L
T E C R T S D A N M L L O O R B R B R B A
O M R Q E A Y A L P F Z K H T M O M L N M
P E I R L S T M L R T I M N S H P U D I P
B R M F U C I E M I E S H I M Y B N E S O
B G E E N L A R G E R V R L E N S F T E P
W E I S D E B R Z C T K O E L E S A E R H
E D D I E A D A M S S R A R R A Y E N Y O
K Z I Z R R H O Y A S L Y A L I G H T Y T
S Z J N E R V S M X T E L P P C F V I E O
H O U E X O M A X O P G P O R P I R G P G
O O F E P S A G T N I C A D E G C N T U R
O M G R O H T F X I O G O O V L J I R O A
T K J C S A R A W M V I O O I A C K A L P
K L I S E K I R I S A E S H E S O O C T H
R B X T D E X P O S U R E E W S X C K N Y
```

Photography Word List #6

Agfa	Gitzo	Mode	Screen
Analog	Glare	Mount	Scrim
Array	Glass	NiCad	Set
Back up	Gobo	Noise	Shade
Backdrop	Grid	Optical	Shake
Beam	Grip	Optics	Shim
Blur	Haze	Overlay	Shoe
Bulb	Hood	Pan	Shoot
Canon	Hot lamp		Silk
Cokin	Hoya	Photography	Skew
Cookie	Ilford	Play	Stop
Cove	Iris	Pop	Strobe
Crop	Kit		Symmetry
Detent	Light	Preservative	Tamrac
Easel	Linhof		Track
Eddie Adams	Loupe	Preview	
Enlarger	Magnifying	Profoto	Underexposed
Exposure		Prop	VR lens
F number	Mask	Raw	Weston
Fire	Matrix	Reflect	Zoom
Flag	Menu	Resin	
Fuji	Merge	Riser	
Gel	Minox	Rotate	
		Sanyo	

Photography #7

```
Y V G K M J A B S S E R P E R P I R S B H
T Y A R N A M N O I T C U D O R P E R M E
M Y L G O B O O H O U T T A K E V O C U K
O E F H F E R I F R M R L I T H I U M L A
D K S A M A H S E I R I S E L U O J I T H
E W U U S V C E L N A D A R L E Y S I I S
L O R U N R I F A C Q M R N I R N E W C P
I L V U I E O P C A O A H S F U I S I O G
N I E M L R M F S N W A K T E S E T R A N
G N I A D B L M E D Z L I H Y H P C E T I
Y H L Y S A G T K E N L T A E O C O T E M
H O L T R E O X A S X E R A P E E Q T D A
O F A E I O L M D C W R L S I D I G A S R
O N N W N X M S O E A B L B E N E C M M F
D T C E S E A E K N E M U L C N O E I Y F
S P E T E N P S M T M U C P E K O N L R U
P I E D Y O T O P S D I R G I R O T A B T
E T G O A N H W S U C A R N M X R M D C M
E C E G G C R A T E H I L R O O E U Q I V
D H E R B R I T T S P R O T O C O L H R M
C L W G A L E N R O W E L L Z R G S A G L
```

Photography Word List #7

Agfa

Array

Bleed

Blend

Blur

Boom

Canon

Chroma

Cokin

Cove

Crop

Easel

Egg crate

Ernst Haas

Eyepiece

F stop

Fill

Fire

Flag

Flare

Frame

Framing

Galen Rowell

Gel

Gobo

Gridspot

Grip

Haze

Herb Ritts

Hood

Hurrell

Ilford

Incandescent

Iris

Joule

Kit

Kodak

Lens

Linhof

Lithium

Low key

Lumen

Man Ray

Mask

Matte

Memory

Menu

Midtone

Minox

Mirror

Modeling

Multicoated

Nadar

NiCad

Niepce

Noise

One to one

Optics

Outtake

Pan

Pitch

Pixel

Pose

Prepress

Protocol

Raw

Reproduction

Rinse

Sanyo

Scale

Scrim

Set

Shake

Sharp

Shim

Shoe

Silk

Skew

Speed

Stand

Surveillance

Umbrella

Weegee

Xenon

Zoom

Photography #8

```
T M O K F D Y T C E J B U S G G L A R E A
O M O R O T F P L O U P E R W E E G E E R
H O T O O N S I L L U M I N A T I O N Y E
S O H P R K I O L A T P I G H O N P D P M
P B Z A P K K C H L Y V P G M M F A G F A
A L O Q Z V R I A G B R I M L E I C A I C
N J O U L E B A N D W L N S A R N I N R R
S A M E M O R Y D A T E U V A L I T R E O
M A P P I N G Q C A M N S B M N T Y A D P
C O V E M A N G O U N S E P O E Y O W E A
H O Y A D N I W L I A S L T E M D O H Y S
P R I S M A M E O R R B F A E E F O G E T
R R K E J L A K R I R L J T H D D Y M E E
F E E L K O R S I S A U E S N I R R S T L
N S L Z Y G F D N G Y R D U N E M H I B J
C I T E I T N E G A T I V E T N O K I N A
H N K O A R L L M E R G E T O E F U J I G
R P R O P S A A K G A E A T B U R N I N G
O P T I C S E L Y U C B S C O R E T I N A
M A T Y S B I C O O K I E I G E R A L F X
A L B U M S E P O P R I N T R E A D I N G
```

Photography Word List #8

Agfa	Fuji	Lumen	Prop
Album	Gel	Mapping	Raw
Analog	Ghost	Mat	Reading
Array	Glare	Memory	Red eye
Battery	Glass	Menu	Release
Beam	Gobo	Merge	Remote
Blur	Grid	Meter	Resin
Boom	Grip	Modem	Retina
Bulb	Halsman	Nadar	Rinse
Burning		Negative	Riser
Camera	Handcoloring	NiCad	Royalty
Chroma	Haze	Nikkor	Sailwind
Cokin	Hood	Nikon	Sanyo
Cookie	Hot lamp	Opacity	Set
Cove	Hoya	Opaque	Shoe
Crop		Optics	Silk
Darkroom	Illumination	Pan	Skew
Detent	Infinity	Pastel	Snapshot
Easel	Iris	Pigment	Snoot
F stop	Joule	Play	Speed ring
Fill	Kit	Polarizer	Subject
Fire	Konica	Pop	Track
Flag	Leica	Print	VR lens
Flare	Light	Prism	Weegee
Framing	Loupe	Proof	Zoom

Photography #9

```
F L A R E T I H W R O N I M E I K O O C Z
S I C A I C R O P L I P U P S N N I K O N
H N R N G S R Y R S E V I T I S O P O P L
O H E A I R E A E N T I K T X U I M S M U
E O N L Y C I R V I Z G S A A C T Z A D M
A F E O M U A D I T K L I S F O C T L O I
R P M G A L F D S R D D D I F F U S E O E
C U U T R A C K U A E O N W O A D G S H R
H P L E Z A H N A M S L A H F R O T A T E
I T L B S A F I L L O R S R I R R T E F N
V T O A V O C G I U P L A N E A P N T J I
E N O O Y T L I Z A X M O D E Y E E N R L
L U M I N A N C E P E Y E C U P R C I R S
C O V E S S I E Z L R A C O L O R S O E U
M M F U J I O V E R E X P O S U R E P C M
G S O B O G S D P E D I S A N Y O D A E A
C L I C K A H R S D N K T A N C I N S D G
N I A R G L A R E H U P O R P M B A T E F
S K E W P H K X O E A L P D A A E C E E A
G G L A S S E L N A N D E G A S A N L P S
F L U I D H E A D D W E E G Y K M I U S R
```

Photography Word List #9

Agfa

Analog

Archive

Array

Beam

Blur

Carl Zeiss

Click

Closeup

Color

Cookie

Cove

Crop

Diffuse

Easel

Eye cup

Fill

Flag

Flare

Fluid head

Focus

Frame

Fuji

Gel

Glare

Glass

Gobo

Grain

Grid

Halsman

Haze

Hood

Hoya

Image

Incandescent

Iris

Kit

Kodak

Leica

Lens

Linhof

Lumen

Lumiere

Luminance

Mask

Mat

Media

Menu

Minor White

Mode

Mount

Muslin

NiCad

Nikon

Off axis

Overexposure

Pan

Pastel

Paul Martin

Pinhole

Plane

Play

Point

Pop

Positive

Previsualize

Prism

Prop

Pupil

Raw

Recede

Redhead

Reproduction

Resin

Riser

Rotate

SanDisk

Sanyo

Set

Shade

Shake

Sharp

Shoe

Silk

Skew

Snoot

Speed

Stop

Track

Underexposed

Zoom

Photography #10

```
T A L E F N R W E K S E G G C R A T E Y T
I N P R L O R E D E Y E C U P O L E S A E
K E A A O N E M S I L A E R O T O H P L S
W M S L O A V H I I E O S Z T A P S H P M
E U T G D C I M O N R C U I S T P I O E Q
I L E M L M T U Y B O P N P R E M R T T H
H N L I A E A B N N O X I A E I O E O C T
E I C M M R V L A E S G U D N E R I F P H
K K O A P G R A S T M H D O P I R T L B G
O O N I N E E M F S A C L E N S M A E E I
B C T D M D S G D G D T O G K O N U X A L
S Q A E A I E I J N A A V B L E N D L M K
A P X M N B R S R U L B N E E R C S F L K
I E A Q R G P C C T E U I U C D I O I R I
L G C N A H G M S E S L K Q R R O S N E S
W R G E Y N O I S E N B O A O R Y M N D H
I I A C I N O R B M A T N P P P A Y O H O
N P X M O P T I C A L Z O O M F R S N E E
D M A P P L E T H O R P E F L A R E E A R
M R O Y S T R Y K E R N S T H A A S X D A
F D H E Y R O M E M V N I A R G L A S S W
```

Photography Word List #10

Agfa	Flood lamp	Media	Proof
Album	Frame	Memory	Prop
Ansel Adams	Framing	Menu	Raw
Array	Gel	Merge	Red eye
Batch	Glare	Metering	Redhead
Beam	Glass	Minolta	Riser
Blend	Gobo	Minox	Rotate
Blur	Grain	Mode	Roy Stryker
Bokeh	Grid	Monopod	Sailwind
Boom	Grip	Nikon	Sanyo
Bronica	Hoya	Noise	Screen
Bulb	Illuminance	Opaque	Scrim
Canon		Optical zoom	Sensor
Click	Incandescent	Pan	Set
Cokin	Iris	Pastel	Shim
Contax	Kit	Photoflex	Shoe
Crop	Lens		Sigma
Easel	Light	Photorealism	Silk
Egg crate	Loupe	Pitch	Skew
Ernst Haas	Lumen	Plane	Speed
Eye cup	Man Ray	Play	Stop
Eyepiece		Pop	Tripod
Fire	Mapplethorpe		Tungsten
Flare	Mat	Preservative	Xenon

Photography #11

```
T C I G L A S S Z P L N S T O P Y M M I V
G N I T T E U O H L I S P E I A E I E A X
J B I N S A O O L S P H R N L K H G M N T
B L B O O M T I E S U V O P A S T E L S U
L U P I P O F R S E P N O O B R O N I C A
O R O S N E S L A T E P F Y D R L U M E N
W G V E O V E R E X P O S U R E S I R A W
N O R M A N L I G H T R B O G T B L E E D
O G L T N O Z I R O H T E Y R T E M M Y S
U W E K S A E C I A G F A N O U P P O R P
T Z N Y V K P G P L I O M A Y H R U T E T
M A S K A S R L Y B L L D S A S O N E P R
R U O H C I G A M U P I R Y L A H E A U I
E M S Y D R F R M M O O O A T L T P G O P
S O E S N I R E S W T H F R Y F E O A L O
G N I R P E T S L I E S L R R R L C B O D
S H O O T E R I H E X E I A S D P O D N H
S R R B R B U L B A D A G A Z A P V N G E
H C T I P C O K I N Z O F E R C A E A O A
O S N I E P C E M O D E M F E I M L S B D
E G H O S T D E F I N I T I O N F M Z O T
```

Photography Word List #11

Agfa

Album

Array

Beam

Bleed

Blown out

Blur

Boom

Bronica

Bulb

Cokin

Cove

Crop

Definition

Easel

Fill

Flag

Flash

Gel

Ghost

Glare

Glass

Gobo

Grid

Grip

Haze

Hood

Horizon

Hoya

Ilford

Iris

Kit

Loupe

Lumen

Magic hour

Mapplethorpe

Mask

Mat

Menu

Metering

Model

Modem

NiCad

Niepce

Noise

Norman Light

Off axis

Open up

Overexposure

Pan

Paper safe

Pastel

Photon

Pitch

Play

Point

Pop

Portfolio

Pose

Proof

Prop

Pupil

Raw

Remote

Resin

Rinse

Riser

Royalty

Sandbag

Sanyo

Sensor

Set

Shake

Shim

Shoe

Shooter

Shutter

Silhouetting

Silk

Skew

Step ring

Stop

Symmetry

Top light

Tripod head

VR lens

Weegee

Xenon

Zoom

Photography #12

```
S F A I D E M S C T R A C K P Z L I G H T
E D R U V M S C H K S S O L G I M E S E N
N I S O S A T R R E V I H C R A X A N P L
S R C Q N R U I O D Q A L V G Z T E O S R
O G R Y U F D M M H R E T E M S I P L P E
R A O L E Z I L A U S I V E R P K F I U G
W Y B K G N O R K A H A Z E A A R G V P N
Y A L P O T J G E N A M L O G M M A X I I
D R Z L F O R N Y J D A U F O E G Y H L F
T N T O U V F I L T E R A B N A O I E S T
Q A P B O F N S P B N U N T L E Q C S V U
X M M O M M O U S O O E S F N A P P R M F
H R Q G E O T C P K D P Y H I E B O B O M
M O O B D O S O P W E M N S I B A T C H P
P K Y Y O R E F I B V W O N S M Y S Y D Q
R K E A M K W N L B A C K U P O A F E E K
E I L R W R L E D M P R L D N O L E H T G
V N A R O A N V A A R R R I O T R G O E I
I N C A N D E S C E N T I E C A E P O N T
E N S D S I L K I B U L B S L K V P D T Z
W I D E O P E N N I K O N G M C O L O R O
```

Photography Word List #12

Agfa

Album

Archive

Array

Avedon

Back up

Barrel

Batch

Beam

Blend

Blur

Boom

Bulb

Chromakey

Click

Color

Cove

Crop

Darkroom

Detent

Easel

Edwin Land

F stop

Finger

Fire

Flag

Focusing

Frame

Gel

Gitzo

Glare

Glossy

Gobo

Grid

Haze

Hood

Hoya

Image

Incandescent

Iris

Kit

Lens

Light

Man Ray

Mat

Media

Meter

Minolta

Modem

NiCad

Niepce

Nikkor

Nikon

Open flash

Overlay

Pan

Pigment

Pixel

Play

Pop

Preview

Previsualize

Prism

Prop

Pupil

Raw

Sanyo

Scale

Scrim

Semigloss

Sensor

Set

Shade

Sharp

Shim

Sigma

Silk

Skew

Snow mode

Studio

Track

Tripod mount

UV filter

Weston

Wide open

Zoom

Photography #13

```
Q J H E J B F I P D V G S C A L E C L R D
V M D U B L J G E R P R C N C M O E M O C
E E A Q P U C E Y E O I A P I V G O D L N
X S C A F B P A K C S P U N E P O B O O M
T U I P J S C A C S N S B C L R O S M C M
E F N O T I H C I S A E E L K W E S T O N
N F N P N S C U R V E M R R U U I T E K S
S I L O I D R S T A N D A A P R O O F I Z
I D R T I N O I T C U D O R P E R J R N O
O B N R F T P O A G F A T V J S R I V A O
N A G I R D A E H D E R S G E H N P S X M
R X R E W A X S C I T P O O N R H A Z E G
E E A B S E D P N S J K H J F I L L R O R
B O N T S N R A K E L I G H T T M I L T O
M H O H N A I E N G P T N E D S B A G X T
U S I B H O W R F R A M E C R I N O R H A
N M T S J O C U L A R L O S I A G E X F T
F E A T N E T E D I X E S C D D L I L R E
L M L A R F C O K N U X I M A G E G T K N
A K A L I A R T T H G I L F O R D N S A B
G I H T R M W S E T U P K O D A K K T X L
```

Photography Word List #13

Agfa

Analog

Anti shake

Blur

Boom

Bronica

Bulb

Closeup

Cokin

Color

Compensation

Contax

Cove

Crop

Darkroom

Detent

Diffuse

Digital

Extension

Eye cup

F number

Fill

Fire

Flag

Frame

Framing

Fuji

Gel

Ghost

Glare

Grain

Grid

Grip

Halation

Hat trick

Haze

Hood

Ilford

Image

Incident

Iris

Kit

Kodak

Leica

Lens

Light trail

Mask

Mat

Mode

Nadar

NiCad

Noise

Object

Ocular

Opaque

Open up

Optics

Overlight

Pan

Pixel

Pop

Pose

Prepress

Prism

Proof

Prop

Rake light

Raw

Redhead

Reproduction

Rewind

Rinse

Riser

Rotate

S curve

Scale

Setup

Sharp

Shim

Shoe

Silk

Skew

Softbox

Speed

Stand

Transparency

Weston

Zoom

Photography #14

```
L X P U P I L U X H M F D E G A T R A C K
T O T I U O O A V A G O I E Y V V N W N R
P G R I D G K P Y X T O O R E E C J I E Y
H G A S G N N E M U L N B B E P N O T R H
O O N E T I M E U S E O E O L A S E V K P
T F S A A R R A Y T G I H P D U M R E E A
O M P S M O U N T S B S P A U M B M N R R
E A A E R L N A C G U E R F I O B O O E G
S G R L O O M O M H R C O N V D L O I D O
S N E F N C I T U O N W O L B E E Z S E H
A I N A I D G M W S I X F F H M N T N Y T
Y F C S U N P B E T N A B L E O D I E E I
P Y Y T I A E O K N G B F A B D Y G T N L
M L S D X H T A S W U Q L G W E T A X F T
M A A K I T O P R E V I S U A L I Z E K K
E E S Y F N M U I T M E M O R Y C A R D D
R O K K I N E K E Y L I G H T P A L S L N
G S N E L O R C A M F L A S O R P B S E A
E O C U L A R A F P A Z I T V O O U H I T
D O P O N O M B A R E L S I X P D M I C S
C E L L P H O N E Y K A X O E A S T M A N
```

Photography Word List #14

Agfa

Album

Array

Back up

Blend

Blown out

Blur

Boom

Bulb

Burning

Canon

Cell phone

Cove

Crop

Defocus

Detent

Easel

Eastman

Extension

Fill

Fine art

Fire

Flag

Gel

Ghost

Gitzo

Glare

Gobo

Green eye

Grid

Grip

Handcoloring

Haze

Hood

Hoya

Key light

Kit

Leica

Lithography

Loupe

Lumen

Macro lens

Magnify

Mask

Matte

Memory card

Menu

Merge

Meter

Minox

Model

Modem

Monopod

Mount

Nadar

Nikkor

Noise

Ocular

One time use

Opacity

Pan

Pentax

Photo essay

Play

Pop

Pose

Previsualize

Print

Proof

Prop

Pupil

Raw

Reading

Red eye

Remote

Set

Shim

Shoe

Silk

Skew

Speed

Stand

Stop

Studio

Tamron

Track

Transparency

Zoom

Photography #15

```
P S P A C I E L G A T E F O L D P P L P F
U N O A F G A S N O O T U A R R A Y E R I
P E P S H U T T E R B N J X O B T H G I L
I L O V E R R I D E L O I R Y P T W R N M
L R S A C R O P M S K I A M N G E Y I T S
F E I P N M S A X I S T E A A K R N D E P
O T N E A D E H I N I A Z Q S G N Q U R E
C L G R L B Y D A V L Z A M B I E N T P E
U I S T L A Y W I R K I H O T S P O T L D
S F T U I Y C V A A P R O O F I H N M A T
I T O R E F R S M R I A Y W A R S A X Y N
N S O E V N I A R G H L A F E I A C K M G
G A L F R I S R T D R O F L I E L M U E N
E R I G U K E E E N S P L N V L F B E X I
D T U O S O R T V H E I N R I C L I C K M
O N R L R N Q E I O M M U M G A T M Z K A
M O Y A R N A M N E C C U T N E T E D O R
X C D N L S B B E O S P U C E Y E R K N F
N A P A E U L L K P N I K K O R T G U I Y
N K N L L U C I R E D E Y E T D O E D C T
S E T B R H N O V E R E X P O S U R E A Z
```

Photography Word List #15

Agfa

Album

Ambient

Analog

Andy Warhol

Aperture

Array

Beam

Blur

Bulb

Canon

Click

Cokin

Contrast

Cove

Crop

Curtain

Detent

Documentary

Easel

Eye cup

Fill

Film speed

Filter

Fire

Flag

Focusing

Frame

Framing

Fuji

Gatefold

Gel

Gobo

Grain

Grid

Haze

Hot spot

Hoya

Ilford

Image

Iris

Kit

Konica

Lee Miller

Leica

Lens

Light box

Man Ray

Mask

Mat

Media

Merge

Meter

Mode

Nadar

Nikkor

Nikon

Ocular

Open up

Overexposure

Override

Pan

Pattern

Play

Polarization

Pop

Posing stool

Printer

Proof

Pupil

Raw

Red eye

Resin

Riser

S curve

Sanyo

Scale

Set

Shake

Sharp

Shim

Shutter

Silk

Skew

Snoot

Surveillance

TTL flash

Vivitar

Xenon

Photography #16

```
E Z A H M E N U D S C R E W M O U N T L T
O Y O R U O H C I G A M B I E N T G R I P
N A P O P H S T R I N G E R N S T H A A S
O L T R M S Y A G O F E N I L S U M L F S
I P O Y H O I W D O L Y M P U S W I U L I
S P H I S N B E B A T T E R Y E E P C E X
E H M A P S V J I G H Y V X K N V H O T A
P U T E S A O D E G L E N S A W P O T S F
R R E G L E E L I C I S F L A G E T C A F
I R A A X M O L G L T U P R L E D O M P O
N E R M C O M N L Q J F P I X E L G M N B
T L S I R I B A E I L F O R D K D R I I O
I L H P R I N T E R F I C N C C E A C E G
N G E B N C I O F S E D A G F A T P L P T
G L E U E S K P R O N T M F I R E H O C C
I A T S T R O B E B S I E Y U T N E S E E
M R M U Z S N S C O L O R C A S T R E K J
C E D E E L B I S I G M A B A R E B U L B
R I O D U O B L A C K L I G H T R D P P U
O P A Q U E C K U I G O R D O N P A R K S
P B R E T E M A T R I X P R O O F B O O K
```

Photography Word List #16

Agfa

Ambient

Array

Avedon

Barebulb

Battery

Beam

Black light

Bleed

Blur

Boudoir

Bronica

Camera

Closeup

Color cast

Cove

Crop

Curtain

Detent

Diffuse

Ernst Haas

F stop

Fill

Fire

Flag

Fuji

Glare

Glossy

Gobo

Gordon Parks

Grain

Grid

Grip

Haze

Hurrell

Ilford

Image

Iris

Kit

Lens

Magic hour

Matrix

Media

Menu

Meter

Model

Muslin

Niepce

Nikon

Noise

Object

Ocular

Off axis

Olympus

Opaque

Pan

Pastel

Phase One

Photographer

Pixel

Plane

Play

Pop

Pose

Printer

Printing

Proof book

Prop

Raw

Rim light

Rinse

Screw mount

Setup

Shim

Shoe

Sigma

Silk

Skew

Softbox

Stand

Stringer

Strobe

Studio

Subject

Surveillance

Tear sheet

Track

Zoom

Photography #17

```
L I N U K E W V Z W T L J R H O Y A V S B
S U F L A R E W E W E L P M A S E R E I O
N H M E N U O E T G S C A N N E R H G R U
E R O I C T Y S A M A E B J D S G R A I N
L K E T N R N T R A C K H J C I R E M Z C
L P K T S E A O C H C T A B O G I U I A E
E U O S T P S N G C R Y T M L M D Q N P C
N C T I A A O C G D I O C E O A Y A I I A
O E L L N M P T E M O K V A R O Q P K R R
T Y O K D T H F A N M O D E M L B O O G D
A E D H L Y O M S P C O F I R E D P N S T
I P G D S C N P R H P E Z N D D R U P I N
P M F A U C O O K I E P T K U O S A K I R
E O I S L M O R R D E R H L G M N S A E L
S S L H F F F T D N X O S R A B B B T T M O
D A L B U M K R T N O M A S J L R E M O U
A I P E J P L A Y D I M L Z D U M F R O P
C C G R I X X I E K A W F W C B T R Q Z E
I R O N O C O T R P Y R E T T A B A G F A
N O B F N P A D A G U E R R E Q F M M F H
Q P O E E G E E W S N A P S H O T E K X M
```

Photography Word List #17

Agfa	Flag	Mamiya	Raw
Album	Flare	Mask	Resample
Aperture	Frame	Mat	Rewind
Batch	Fuji	Menu	Samsung
Battery	Gel	Meter	Sanyo
Beam	Gobo	Model	Scanner
Boom	Grain	Modem	Sepia tone
Bounce card	Grid	Mosaic	Set
Bulb mode	Grip	Muddy	Shoe
Camera	Handcolor	NiCad	Sigma
Cookie	Haze	Nikon	Silk
Cove	Hood	Opaque	Snapshot
Crop	Hot spot	Pan	Snoot
Curtain	Hoya	Pattern	Stand
Daguerre	Image	Pentax	Stop
Defocus	Iris	Play	Track
Egg crate	Kit	Point	Tripod
Eye cup	Leica	Pop	Weegee
F number	Lens	Portrait	Weston
Fill	Loupe	Preflash	Zoom
Fire	Luminescence	Program	
		Proof	
		Prop	

Photography #18

```
S G C H S A L F P U P O P N I K O C O S Y
C Y D D U M P H O T O N N F L E S Y R A D
K O N I G H T P H O T O O L N G R H L O O
L P L C B S U R V E I L L A N C E P I J P
I E Q O D U M O Y S E R L G S S T A J M O
N N S P R E L Q E I N P C L I C K R N O N
H U B A O D L B C O R S U N F S I G M A O
O P U D E W V A K Q V E E O E S P O R P M
F N I E P C E I Y D T M T B L I T T L E G
V R L E N S N R E N U W U I M L S O V J X
G B A U E Z Z E U L G C D A N K C H O O D
L D V W F X P O C P H E G S S A R P N H N
K S A M R S M R M S V E U G N F I I E F S
J B E D A H S P A I E C B O O I M E T E R
X O C I M O M L E H O N N R O R G N E P J
Y O P O E E F W B F S F I L T E R L K R E
A M B P S N E L T S A F V M E L U A D I S
G N A T U R E P H O T O S W U O I R X S T
F P R E F L A S H M E N U K J L R G T M O
A M I R R O R S L A P V A X E Y I E H A P
E I K O O C S Y R R U L B P B W S R E T Y
```

Photography Word List #18

Agfa

Beam

Bleed

Blurry

Boom

Bulb

Canon

Click

Cokin

Color

Cookie

Crop

Diopter

Easel

Enlarger

Fast lens

Filter

Fire

Flag

Flash cube

Focus

Frame

Gel

Grid

Hood

Image

Iris

Joule

Kit

Leica

Light

Linhof

Loupe

Lumen

Luminescence

Mask

Mat

Menu

Meter

Minox

Mirror slap

Monopod

Mount

Muddy

Nature photo

Niepce

Night photo

Nikon

Noise

Open up

Pan

Photography

Photon

Plane

Play

Pop up flash

Power up

Preflash

Prism

Prop

Raw

Retina

Scrim

Set

Shade

Sharp

Shim

Shoe

Shoot

Sigma

Silk

Skew

Slide viewer

Snoot

Softbox

Speed

Stop

Surveillance

Sync delay

VR lens

Weegee

Photography #19

```
H F M F L A G N I R S U C O F F L E N S C
C S U E X T E N S I O N A Q O X L F K I T
T J S R E P R O D U C T I O N U R B A E C
I G L A R E L N H B L U R B O E O S S P O
P U P I L E D A K O F P O J L O O E D O M
N O N E X G S C N L Y R T E M M Y S A L P
E T I I V D I I A C E A A C G L C S C A O
G C P M E L M S O D O S T T R R T N I R S
A S L E C X H P E N E L E H I O E N N O I
T D L M K C L C U L D E O M P V F M E I T
I B I O A A E N E R M T A R Z I I K C D E
V G F R Y R E S I R S S J C N P A V A D W
E H D Y G M N V E H K A I I O T A M R O N
Z O O M M A I D O K L P T R T K N R C G E
A S N O O T N E Y C I Y C U P O I U Y R T
V T U O R I E N T A T I O N K N L N I A H
S N O K F B T R L R H I R I S A O F M Y A
T I L L U M I N A T I O N E R H W P S C Z
G Y L L I P G G Y S U R S R P R K K O A E
M E B K O P F Q O V M O A A O A E M A R F
H O L D B A C K R K P Y N E Z W Y S G D P
```

Photography Word List #19

Agfa

Array

Asymmetry

Bleed

Blur

Boom

Bulb

Canon

Click

Cokin

Color

Composite

Cove

Crop

Easel

Extension

Fill

Finder

Fire

Flag

Flash card

Focus ring

Frame

Fuji

Gel

Ghost

Glare

Glass

Gray card

Grid

Grip

Haze

Hold back

Hot shoe

Hoya

Illumination

Infinity

Iris

Joule

Kit

Leica

Lens

Lithium

Low key

Mask

Mat

Memory

Menu

Merge

Minolta

Mode

Mosaic

Mount

Negative

NiCad

Nikon

Noise

Object

Ocular

Orientation

Outtake

Pan

Pastel

Pitch

Pixel

Play

Polaroid

Pose

Print

Prism

Proof

Prop

Pupil

Raw

Recede

Release

Reproduction

Rinse

Riser

Rotate

Royalty

Scrim

Set

Silk

Skew

Snoot

Stop

Tamrac

Tamron

Track

Tripod

Vivitar

Xenon

Zoom

Photography #20

```
M E R G E M B L U R A L D I K H F O C U S
S O E S N O O T S X C P O S E K O N I C A
T T T E W T K D Y C I Y E K E L D D I M S
R O L U M I E R E V E R S E E E O E D F A R
I F I Q S P H F A M L P M K K S H V M O Z
N O F A N Y H L I G H T S A N D I S K B D
G R V P E S B O S L O W F I L M U K S J V
E P U O L U N A T V L R R U B N I D T E F
R J C S M W W E B O O M M M G N I C O C L
Z L H R O P E K L S M E T E R O E I P T A
Z I I D O Z K A N L N O B N L I L H L U G
M D A I Z P S E S X A E N U U S U A A G I
D H N B M A S K T T A C L T R E O Z N R R
S T E S E E V P R M M L O K A S J E E A I
W T M H G R I P O B E A Y F D G I L B I S
E N A A F D R D B C C O N C A V E L E N S
E E M K N L O A E N I C A D N A U M K M R
G I S E A R A O T K I T S F S B P R O P L
E B F F A Y A S H I C A I E C A N O N E X
E M G W P L A Y H G O R L D N E L B G D J
T A M R O N I K O N E N T O P S D I R G I
```

Photography Word List #20

Aberration

Afocal lens

Agfa

Album

Ambient

Analog

Beam

Blend

Blur

Bokeh

Boom

Bulb

Canon

Celluloid

Concave lens

Crop

Easel

Eastman

Fill

Fire

Flag

Flash

Focus

Gel

Grain

Gridspot

Grip

Haze

Hood

Image sensor

Iris

Joule

Kit

Konica

Leica

Lensbaby

Light

Loupe

Lumen

Lumiere

Man Ray

Mask

Mat

Menu

Merge

Meter

Middle key

Modem

Nadar

NiCad

Nikkor

Nikon

Noise

Object

Opaque

Pan

Photomontage

Plane

Play

Point

Pose

Profoto

Prop

Raw

Release

Reverse

Rinse

Samsung

SanDisk

Sanyo

Set

Shadow

Shake

Shim

Shoe

Silk

Skew

Slow film

Snoot

Stop

Stringer

Strobe

Tamron

UV filter

Weegee

Xenon

Yashica

Zoom lens

Word Scramble

PHOTO TERMS

PEULO

_ _ _ _ _

SIFUERDF

_ _ _ _ _ _ _ _

FEETRLACECN

_ _ _ _ _ _ _ _ _ _ _

IFLM FSEA

_ _ _ _ _ _ _ _ _

AHFSL RADC

_ _ _ _ _ _ _ _ _ _

CLFOA LPEAN

_ _ _ _ _ _ _ _ _ _ _

NLCEEEARF

_ _ _ _ _ _ _ _ _

HGSOT

_ _ _ _ _

OSSRC IHGLT

_ _ _ _ _ _ _ _ _ _ _

OAACFL NLSE

_ _ _ _ _ _ _ _ _ _

ASENSIETEDT

_ _ _ _ _ _ _ _ _ _ _

RVEFIIDEWN

_ _ _ _ _ _ _ _ _ _

PHOTO TERMS

MAASENT

_ _ _ _ _ _ _

URNGIBN

_ _ _ _ _ _ _

WLO TCNOTSAR

_ _ _ _ _ _ _ _ _ _ _

MLIF DSEPE

_ _ _ _ _ _ _ _ _

LASFH UECB

_ _ _ _ _ _ _ _

LFCOA OIPTN

_ _ _ _ _ _ _ _ _ _

EREEFZ OFCSU

_ _ _ _ _ _ _ _ _ _

NSEL AREFL

_ _ _ _ _ _ _ _ _

OLOP HGITL

_ _ _ _ _ _ _ _ _

EETDRAUATS

_ _ _ _ _ _ _ _ _ _

TBINMEA

_ _ _ _ _ _ _

ATILYDHG

_ _ _ _ _ _ _ _

PHOTO TERMS

UNLLNAIIIOTM   _ _ _ _ _ _ _ _ _ _ _ _

FLUETYBTR   _ _ _ _ _ _ _ _ _

TSAF ELNS   _ _ _ _ _ _ _ _ _

EFRIGN   _ _ _ _ _ _

CRONBAI   _ _ _ _ _ _ _

OUFCS TFSIH   _ _ _ _ _ _ _ _ _ _ _

LLFU EGNLTH   _ _ _ _ _ _ _ _ _ _

LGSAS   _ _ _ _ _

CTENIHORGU   _ _ _ _ _ _ _ _ _ _

REGNE EEY   _ _ _ _ _ _ _ _ _

PRIG   _ _ _ _

IRAH IHTGL   _ _ _ _ _ _ _ _ _

Puzzle #4
PHOTO TERMS

NAIRBTRAEO   _ _ _ _ _ _ _ _ _ _

ROLOC ACTS   _ _ _ _ _ _ _ _ _

LNTAGEMENER   _ _ _ _ _ _ _ _ _ _ _

ILBL NARBDT   _ _ _ _ _ _ _ _ _ _

LUDLLOECI   _ _ _ _ _ _ _ _ _

TSTAOROOPH   _ _ _ _ _ _ _ _ _ _

DAYN HLROWA   _ _ _ _ _ _ _ _ _ _

EFLTIR   _ _ _ _ _ _

RNBA ROSOD   _ _ _ _ _ _ _ _ _

CBTAH   _ _ _ _ _

OOWLRPE   _ _ _ _ _ _ _

IFRLEPO   _ _ _ _ _ _ _

PHOTO TERMS

EEY PCU   _ _ _ _ _ _

ELSN LENMETE   _ _ _ _ _ _ _ _ _ _ _

HGLTI ETNT   _ _ _ _ _ _ _ _ _

OCOLR LEWHE   _ _ _ _ _ _ _ _ _ _

MTPOOIECS   _ _ _ _ _ _ _ _ _

AOEPRLHPTEMP   _ _ _ _ _ _ _ _ _ _ _

NAVOCEC ENSL   _ _ _ _ _ _ _ _ _ _ _

OMZO   _ _ _ _

RNOMI EHWIT   _ _ _ _ _ _ _ _ _ _

UNEILMCNA   _ _ _ _ _ _ _ _ _

KBCAL ACRD   _ _ _ _ _ _ _ _ _ _

LEBU ECNESR   _ _ _ _ _ _ _ _ _ _ _

PHOTO TERMS

TPEERUAR   _ _ _ _ _ _ _ _

ECVO   _ _ _ _

ORCMA EDOM   _ _ _ _ _ _ _ _ _ _

ITGILHNG   _ _ _ _ _ _ _ _

LBSELOW   _ _ _ _ _ _ _

IGHTL BAETL   _ _ _ _ _ _ _ _ _ _ _

RCOP   _ _ _ _

PCEINE   _ _ _ _ _ _

IOKCN   _ _ _ _ _

ECMAAR KSHEA   _ _ _ _ _ _ _ _ _ _ _

LFIL   _ _ _ _

LFEAR   _ _ _ _ _

PHOTO TERMS

NNOEX

_ _ _ _ _

TDMILAMIUE

_ _ _ _ _ _ _ _ _ _

FOF ISXA

_ _ _ _ _ _ _ _

IEPSPEOSMRU

_ _ _ _ _ _ _ _ _ _ _

GTHAPORPOH

_ _ _ _ _ _ _ _ _ _

IPHCT

_ _ _ _ _

OTAIIZNOLAPR

_ _ _ _ _ _ _ _ _ _ _

FASELHPR

_ _ _ _ _ _ _ _

ROOOPFT

_ _ _ _ _ _ _

ECIUNARLEVLS

_ _ _ _ _ _ _ _ _ _ _

YOIRCTPRCIE

_ _ _ _ _ _ _ _ _ _ _

EMETOR

_ _ _ _ _ _

PHOTO TERMS

LLIF AFLSH

_ _ _ _ _ _ _ _ _ _

EMLUN

_ _ _ _ _

ALOCF NRGEA

_ _ _ _ _ _ _ _ _ _ _

RACOM SNEL

_ _ _ _ _ _ _ _ _ _

LAXEPIMGE

_ _ _ _ _ _ _ _ _

ILSLT OPTOH

_ _ _ _ _ _ _ _ _ _ _

EUDN OTHOP

_ _ _ _ _ _ _ _ _ _

MNPOAARA

_ _ _ _ _ _ _ _

LHDOPOOTOF

_ _ _ _ _ _ _ _ _ _

MIGTPNE

_ _ _ _ _ _ _

YLAP

_ _ _ _

WRPOE PU

_ _ _ _ _ _ _ _

PHOTO TERMS

NOCAN

_ _ _ _ _

EVTSPIIO

_ _ _ _ _ _ _ _

AFST LFMI

_ _ _ _ _ _ _ _ _

NEFI IGARN

_ _ _ _ _ _ _ _ _ _

SHALF ERETM

_ _ _ _ _ _ _ _ _ _ _

SFUCO KOLC

_ _ _ _ _ _ _ _ _ _

LULF AFEMR

_ _ _ _ _ _ _ _ _ _

ELRAG NZEO

_ _ _ _ _ _ _ _ _ _

RUYTRAILGAN

_ _ _ _ _ _ _ _ _ _ _

CELGRYAAS

_ _ _ _ _ _ _ _ _

RDSGIPTO

_ _ _ _ _ _ _ _

DEUGI MNBREU

_ _ _ _ _ _ _ _ _ _ _

PHOTO TERMS

LNOATIAH   _ _ _ _ _ _ _ _

RDHA GHTLI   _ _ _ _ _ _ _ _ _

ZHAE ELRITF   _ _ _ _ _ _ _ _ _ _

RAHOSGTMI   _ _ _ _ _ _ _ _ _

DOOH   _ _ _ _

OTH OTPS   _ _ _ _ _ _ _

TILOMNA   _ _ _ _ _ _ _

YECUHPFORS   _ _ _ _ _ _ _ _ _ _

MIEAG RAEA   _ _ _ _ _ _ _ _ _

ERRLULH   _ _ _ _ _ _ _

TNSNIIETY   _ _ _ _ _ _ _ _ _

LUJEO   _ _ _ _ _

PHOTO TERMS

GTINEHRSSB

_ _ _ _ _ _ _ _ _ _

DN TLRIEF

_ _ _ _ _ _ _ _ _

NGTRFEHIAE

_ _ _ _ _ _ _ _ _ _

EFIR

_ _ _ _

SFAHL WADOHS

_ _ _ _ _ _ _ _ _ _ _

EBWNORI

_ _ _ _ _ _ _

LLFU ESCAL

_ _ _ _ _ _ _ _ _ _

SYLOSG

_ _ _ _ _ _

IGNRA

_ _ _ _ _

TTIGENEV

_ _ _ _ _ _ _ _

MECIARLSYTMA

_ _ _ _ _ _ _ _ _ _ _ _

EBYATTR

_ _ _ _ _ _ _

PHOTO TERMS

RNECTOERV   _ _ _ _ _ _ _ _ _

CNIFOSUG   _ _ _ _ _ _ _ _

IORDNTSOTI   _ _ _ _ _ _ _ _ _ _

XOCNVE NESL   _ _ _ _ _ _ _ _ _ _ _

OEKOIC   _ _ _ _ _ _

OLCO SOOLCR   _ _ _ _ _ _ _ _ _ _

KBGHCLATI   _ _ _ _ _ _ _ _ _

RTMGNIEE   _ _ _ _ _ _ _ _

VENDAO   _ _ _ _ _ _

TLHGI REEMT   _ _ _ _ _ _ _ _ _ _

HALFS NSCY   _ _ _ _ _ _ _ _ _

MECARA   _ _ _ _ _ _

PHOTO TERMS

SAOTCRNT   _ _ _ _ _ _ _ _

MEACAR HONEP   _ _ _ _ _ _ _ _ _ _ _

NKCAOI   _ _ _ _ _ _

NWYN LLKOCUB   _ _ _ _ _ _ _ _ _ _

TLIODGFLHO   _ _ _ _ _ _ _ _ _

OGLYHTRAIHP   _ _ _ _ _ _ _ _ _ _ _

ZSEFISNZU   _ _ _ _ _ _ _ _

OBGO   _ _ _ _

TEHURST   _ _ _ _ _ _ _

DALIBR OPTHO   _ _ _ _ _ _ _ _ _ _ _

LHFAS ENGAR   _ _ _ _ _ _ _ _ _ _

GFO RTFLIE   _ _ _ _ _ _ _ _ _

PHOTO TERMS

NMA AYR   _ _ _ _ _ _

AEHZ   _ _ _ _

IHLGGTIHH   _ _ _ _ _ _ _ _ _

BOMCEYONH   _ _ _ _ _ _ _ _ _

IRONHOZ   _ _ _ _ _ _ _

OTH TGIHL   _ _ _ _ _ _ _ _ _

NUNGIHT   _ _ _ _ _ _ _

EGIAM   _ _ _ _ _

RSETN AHSA   _ _ _ _ _ _ _ _ _ _

ELACI   _ _ _ _ _

SIIR   _ _ _ _

YKE TLGIH   _ _ _ _ _ _ _ _ _

PHOTO TERMS

OLDFIR

_ _ _ _ _ _

LLCE NOEHP

_ _ _ _ _ _ _ _ _ _

RFIUGE DUSTY

_ _ _ _ _ _ _ _ _ _ _ _

OLGN SFCOU

_ _ _ _ _ _ _ _ _ _

IFDLU EADH

_ _ _ _ _ _ _ _ _ _

ONTEHOFERSR

_ _ _ _ _ _ _ _ _ _ _

EAFGRFS AETP

_ _ _ _ _ _ _ _ _ _ _

ELGDON ROHU

_ _ _ _ _ _ _ _ _ _ _

NTHSECIE

_ _ _ _ _ _ _ _

ILGHT VLLEE

_ _ _ _ _ _ _ _ _ _

THLGI EALNP

_ _ _ _ _ _ _ _ _ _

IOLTSUHETE

_ _ _ _ _ _ _ _ _ _

Puzzle #16
PHOTO TERMS

NMRECAOTYUD   _ _ _ _ _ _ _ _ _ _ _

ADRAN   _ _ _ _ _

USDOEFC   _ _ _ _ _ _ _

YBAB HTOSPO   _ _ _ _ _ _ _ _ _ _

IDEAN SUABR   _ _ _ _ _ _ _ _ _ _

GMAIE   _ _ _ _ _

EDEBL   _ _ _ _ _

OOMB   _ _ _ _

OXTANC   _ _ _ _ _ _

EIIDFNOTNI   _ _ _ _ _ _ _ _ _ _

AITRBLNUC   _ _ _ _ _ _ _ _ _

GAFL   _ _ _ _

PHOTO TERMS

EUSTRTH

_ _ _ _ _ _ _

OHAYRKEMC

_ _ _ _ _ _ _ _ _

YRO YKRETRS

_ _ _ _ _ _ _ _ _ _ _

GADCUBNORK

_ _ _ _ _ _ _ _ _ _

PESATC IROTA

_ _ _ _ _ _ _ _ _ _ _

GEAIM ROSNSE

_ _ _ _ _ _ _ _ _ _ _

LNIKEV PETM

_ _ _ _ _ _ _ _ _ _

ECCNTESNANDI

_ _ _ _ _ _ _ _ _ _ _ _

GILHT ELAK

_ _ _ _ _ _ _ _ _ _

LEMIDD AYRG

_ _ _ _ _ _ _ _ _ _

IROEDTP

_ _ _ _ _ _ _

LSEAV NTIU

_ _ _ _ _ _ _ _ _

PHOTO TERMS

OACNBIIRTLA

_ _ _ _ _ _ _ _ _ _ _

IVEW ERMACA

_ _ _ _ _ _ _ _ _ _

DBAOR IGTLH

_ _ _ _ _ _ _ _ _ _

REMTE

_ _ _ _ _

UBLB

_ _ _ _

TAIGCTLHHC

_ _ _ _ _ _ _ _ _ _

THO ESHO

_ _ _ _ _ _ _ _

NLES PEDES

_ _ _ _ _ _ _ _ _ _

NFITYNII

_ _ _ _ _ _ _ _

AOYH

_ _ _ _

ROOGND ARKSP

_ _ _ _ _ _ _ _ _ _ _

TGLHI XBO

_ _ _ _ _ _ _ _ _

PHOTO TERMS

THWAEM RBAYD _ _ _ _ _ _ _ _ _ _ _

OGGDIND _ _ _ _ _ _ _

AACMRE SFHAL _ _ _ _ _ _ _ _ _ _ _

LETFRI AKCP _ _ _ _ _ _ _ _ _ _

SAHLF ILFL _ _ _ _ _ _ _ _ _

CUIEEECNLSNM _ _ _ _ _ _ _ _ _ _ _ _

RNLEFSE SLNE _ _ _ _ _ _ _ _ _ _ _

RGELA _ _ _ _ _

TDERAPA _ _ _ _ _ _ _

TRSETUH RDAG _ _ _ _ _ _ _ _ _ _ _

NETETD _ _ _ _ _ _

UAPL RDSTAN _ _ _ _ _ _ _ _ _ _

PHOTO TERMS

EECTAAT LMFI   _ _ _ _ _ _ _ _ _ _ _

SENL   _ _ _ _

MZOO SNLE   _ _ _ _ _ _ _ _ _

OAANLG   _ _ _ _ _ _

ELFTRI   _ _ _ _ _ _

RRYAA   _ _ _ _ _

SOTUCFOUA   _ _ _ _ _ _ _ _ _

SHBGINERST   _ _ _ _ _ _ _ _ _ _

EHRB ISTRT   _ _ _ _ _ _ _ _ _

MHSALNA   _ _ _ _ _ _ _

LKBAC IHTLG   _ _ _ _ _ _ _ _ _

IMTUHLI   _ _ _ _ _ _ _

PHOTO TERMS

BNAESBLY

_ _ _ _ _ _ _ _

PEDRUESONEX

_ _ _ _ _ _ _ _ _ _ _

IHGTL RUESOC

_ _ _ _ _ _ _ _ _ _ _

CEEIEPEY

_ _ _ _ _ _ _ _

EEONEVGNCCR

_ _ _ _ _ _ _ _ _ _ _

CASBCKTRETA

_ _ _ _ _ _ _ _ _ _ _

OPCY NDTAS

_ _ _ _ _ _ _ _ _ _

GRADFEINNRE

_ _ _ _ _ _ _ _ _ _ _

CPDASLAEN

_ _ _ _ _ _ _ _ _

ELVPEEDOR

_ _ _ _ _ _ _ _ _

GHHI YKE

_ _ _ _ _ _ _ _

DHEDHLAN

_ _ _ _ _ _ _ _

PHOTO TERMS

OYPC NLSE

_ _ _ _ _ _ _ _ _

UCSFO CLKO

_ _ _ _ _ _ _ _ _ _

RGYCIOHPT

_ _ _ _ _ _ _ _ _

AENOFRITRC

_ _ _ _ _ _ _ _ _ _

RLAC ISZSE

_ _ _ _ _ _ _ _ _

NIFE TAR

_ _ _ _ _ _ _ _

ROUEPXSE

_ _ _ _ _ _ _ _

HITGL

_ _ _ _ _

ACBK PU

_ _ _ _ _ _ _

MBEA

_ _ _ _

LAWREK VASEN

_ _ _ _ _ _ _ _ _ _ _

AMREAC YODB

_ _ _ _ _ _ _ _ _ _

PHOTO TERMS

YCSCSOAER

_ _ _ _ _ _ _ _ _

OOLCR

_ _ _ _ _

BALMU

_ _ _ _ _

GONTCAI

_ _ _ _ _ _ _

REUADERG

_ _ _ _ _ _ _ _

TRTPAIRO

_ _ _ _ _ _ _ _

NTHCTMTEAA

_ _ _ _ _ _ _ _ _ _

LHSFA

_ _ _ _ _

XPNEDOUDSEER

_ _ _ _ _ _ _ _ _ _ _ _

ABTYETR PGIR

_ _ _ _ _ _ _ _ _ _ _

FGAA

_ _ _ _

TGESZITLI

_ _ _ _ _ _ _ _ _

PHOTO TERMS

OMSTOPNCIIO   _ _ _ _ _ _ _ _ _ _ _

LAPDRWENECO   _ _ _ _ _ _ _ _ _ _ _

HNILFO   _ _ _ _ _ _

URYBLR   _ _ _ _ _ _

UORRODFENG   _ _ _ _ _ _ _ _ _ _

IXEDF SUFCO   _ _ _ _ _ _ _ _ _ _

TFOLGEAD   _ _ _ _ _ _ _ _

AUMALN DMOE   _ _ _ _ _ _ _ _ _ _

RPTINGNI   _ _ _ _ _ _ _ _

TIINCNDE   _ _ _ _ _ _ _ _

ALUP RMNAIT   _ _ _ _ _ _ _ _ _ _

WLO EYK   _ _ _ _ _ _

PHOTO TERMS

GHLTNTEISUIO

_ _ _ _ _ _ _ _ _ _ _ _

YDBO PCA

_ _ _ _ _ _ _

EFYSEHI NELS

_ _ _ _ _ _ _ _ _ _ _

ACTNRIU

_ _ _ _ _ _ _

EOKHB

_ _ _ _ _

ALLB EHAD

_ _ _ _ _ _ _ _ _

HSLAF LBUB

_ _ _ _ _ _ _ _ _

NSEL UMTON

_ _ _ _ _ _ _ _ _ _

CDAOKBPR

_ _ _ _ _ _ _ _

IBDROUO

_ _ _ _ _ _ _

CEBUON DARC

_ _ _ _ _ _ _ _ _ _

DKKAO

_ _ _ _ _

PHOTO TERMS

TOPSANBROI

_ _ _ _ _ _ _ _ _ _

IADTFCRFINO

_ _ _ _ _ _ _ _ _ _ _

SRUAOOCIRHC

_ _ _ _ _ _ _ _ _ _ _

EDFFUIS

_ _ _ _ _ _ _

MRAOHC

_ _ _ _ _ _

USUOFY RASKH

_ _ _ _ _ _ _ _ _ _ _

LCFOA HLNTGE

_ _ _ _ _ _ _ _ _ _ _

ANBK HLGTI

_ _ _ _ _ _ _ _ _ _

RBLEAR

_ _ _ _ _ _

LAENS SDAMA

_ _ _ _ _ _ _ _ _ _ _

HOIMTARCC

_ _ _ _ _ _ _ _ _

FTOS SCFUO

_ _ _ _ _ _ _ _ _

PHOTO TERMS

ADMTAAET

_ _ _ _ _ _ _ _ _

AYHSIAC

_ _ _ _ _ _ _

FFO AACMRE

_ _ _ _ _ _ _ _ _ _

AEPPR AFES

_ _ _ _ _ _ _ _ _ _

TPAPHGHOYOR

_ _ _ _ _ _ _ _ _ _ _

EPXIL

_ _ _ _ _

RAZEPIOLR

_ _ _ _ _ _ _ _ _

SPERSPRE

_ _ _ _ _ _ _ _

GRMAPRO

_ _ _ _ _ _ _

AORDI EAVSL

_ _ _ _ _ _ _ _ _ _ _

EYMRYSTM

_ _ _ _ _ _ _ _

YSNC OCRD

_ _ _ _ _ _ _ _ _

Puzzle #28
PHOTO TERMS

IUATAORNST

_ _ _ _ _ _ _ _ _ _

UIJF

_ _ _ _

REIFB CTPIOS

_ _ _ _ _ _ _ _ _ _ _

OSTOH

_ _ _ _ _

LOFOD AMLP

_ _ _ _ _ _ _ _ _

OTOF ANCLDE

_ _ _ _ _ _ _ _ _ _ _

LLUF PTSO

_ _ _ _ _ _ _ _ _

AMETT

_ _ _ _ _

SBHEASDLAL

_ _ _ _ _ _ _ _ _ _

ESCOL OSFCU

_ _ _ _ _ _ _ _ _ _ _

GEG TECAR

_ _ _ _ _ _ _ _ _

PTGIFOHROL

_ _ _ _ _ _ _ _ _ _

PHOTO TERMS

NIOKTGNESY   _ _ _ _ _ _ _ _ _ _

THETRUS GLA   _ _ _ _ _ _ _ _ _ _

FAEL HTRSTEU   _ _ _ _ _ _ _ _ _ _

ESLN LCCIER   _ _ _ _ _ _ _ _ _ _

EKRKIC GHTLI   _ _ _ _ _ _ _ _ _ _

OORLAPID   _ _ _ _ _ _ _ _

ENLS LBEARR   _ _ _ _ _ _ _ _ _ _

ENLS NATGOIC   _ _ _ _ _ _ _ _ _ _ _

ITK   _ _ _

AERGL MATOFR   _ _ _ _ _ _ _ _ _ _ _

SENL APC   _ _ _ _ _ _ _ _

SNLE DOHO   _ _ _ _ _ _ _ _ _

PHOTO TERMS

F PSOT   _ _ _ _ _ _

ORFTAM   _ _ _ _ _ _

GNOL NLSE   _ _ _ _ _ _ _ _

CGAMI UHRO   _ _ _ _ _ _ _ _ _

F BENMRU   _ _ _ _ _ _ _

EARMF   _ _ _ _ _

LGE   _ _ _

ELEOTFRCR   _ _ _ _ _ _ _ _ _

MCAFOERO   _ _ _ _ _ _ _ _

IRAFMNG   _ _ _ _ _ _ _

ANEGELTI   _ _ _ _ _ _ _ _

MICRS   _ _ _ _ _

PHOTO TERMS

EERMT   _ _ _ _ _

LIMUSN   _ _ _ _ _ _

YSUOPLM   _ _ _ _ _ _ _

AEPTLS   _ _ _ _ _ _

OEHGPOTARPHR   _ _ _ _ _ _ _ _ _ _ _

YNSC ALDYE   _ _ _ _ _ _ _ _ _ _

OMOZ HSALF   _ _ _ _ _ _ _ _ _

VVEARTESPIER   _ _ _ _ _ _ _ _ _ _ _ _

RAPRMGO EA   _ _ _ _ _ _ _ _ _ _

OMZO NI   _ _ _ _ _ _ _

CRTLAIRNIEE   _ _ _ _ _ _ _ _ _ _ _

OEGAETRPR   _ _ _ _ _ _ _ _ _

PHOTO TERMS

NUME

_ _ _ _

TEOUMIATCDL

_ _ _ _ _ _ _ _ _ _

JOBCTE ELSN

_ _ _ _ _ _ _ _ _ _

DUTIOS SELN

_ _ _ _ _ _ _ _ _ _

NDWWOI ITGHL

_ _ _ _ _ _ _ _ _ _

EPHILON

_ _ _ _ _ _ _

INPOT ORCUSE

_ _ _ _ _ _ _ _ _ _ _

EPWOR OZMO

_ _ _ _ _ _ _ _ _

CSSOPRE ENLS

_ _ _ _ _ _ _ _ _ _ _

JTSCBEU

_ _ _ _ _ _ _

EEEDCR

_ _ _ _ _ _

BTERADNRM

_ _ _ _ _ _ _ _ _

PHOTO TERMS

HEOS

_ _ _ _

HLITG LTRIA

_ _ _ _ _ _ _ _ _ _ _ _

SELCUPO

_ _ _ _ _ _ _

OIZECOLR

_ _ _ _ _ _ _ _

LORCO ACST

_ _ _ _ _ _ _ _ _ _

RCOLO HIFST

_ _ _ _ _ _ _ _ _ _ _

IEDED DSMAA

_ _ _ _ _ _ _ _ _ _

OCFSU

_ _ _ _ _

EEGWEE

_ _ _ _ _ _

TRETBYA ACKP

_ _ _ _ _ _ _ _ _ _ _

EGRNE RSECEN

_ _ _ _ _ _ _ _ _ _ _

LBRU

_ _ _ _

PHOTO TERMS

ONDIGONCRHAL   _ _ _ _ _ _ _ _ _ _ _

THA CRKIT   _ _ _ _ _ _ _ _

NWETOS   _ _ _ _ _ _

LOHD KABC   _ _ _ _ _ _ _ _

ESLN ESHAD   _ _ _ _ _ _ _ _ _

THO AMLP   _ _ _ _ _ _ _

EOSH DRAPTEA   _ _ _ _ _ _ _ _ _ _

NLELNACIIMU   _ _ _ _ _ _ _ _ _ _ _

EMIAG ANLEP   _ _ _ _ _ _ _ _ _ _

NODORI DEMO   _ _ _ _ _ _ _ _ _ _

FLES IRTEM   _ _ _ _ _ _ _ _ _

COLOWTT   _ _ _ _ _ _ _

PHOTO TERMS

OLRICFIMM

_ _ _ _ _ _ _ _ _

NYCS DPSEE

_ _ _ _ _ _ _ _ _ _

OMZO SELN

_ _ _ _ _ _ _ _ _

MOOZ TOU

_ _ _ _ _ _ _ _

RAET TSHEE

_ _ _ _ _ _ _ _ _ _

CTKA APSRH

_ _ _ _ _ _ _ _ _ _

OPP

_ _ _

ERTSPE OCSFU

_ _ _ _ _ _ _ _ _ _ _ _

RPAOGMR ODME

_ _ _ _ _ _ _ _ _ _ _

KAER GITHL

_ _ _ _ _ _ _ _ _ _

LERCYCE MEIT

_ _ _ _ _ _ _ _ _ _ _

DPEORORNCTIU

_ _ _ _ _ _ _ _ _ _ _

PHOTO TERMS

OMYMER

_ _ _ _ _ _

UMDDY

_ _ _ _ _

ETJOBC

_ _ _ _ _ _

TOCSK OHTOP

_ _ _ _ _ _ _ _ _ _ _

OCNOHTPEIG

_ _ _ _ _ _ _ _ _ _

UDOSIT

_ _ _ _ _ _

OPNIT

_ _ _ _ _

RPOWE INDWER

_ _ _ _ _ _ _ _ _ _ _

ORPSNSGICE

_ _ _ _ _ _ _ _ _ _

ITWEH IHLTG

_ _ _ _ _ _ _ _ _ _

EWID NEOP

_ _ _ _ _ _ _ _

NDIW NAMHICE

_ _ _ _ _ _ _ _ _ _

PHOTO TERMS

ETCACN HGTLI   _ _ _ _ _ _ _ _ _ _ _

WRA   _ _ _

RLEGERAN   _ _ _ _ _ _ _ _

GDIAILT   _ _ _ _ _ _ _

ECHVRAI   _ _ _ _ _ _ _

SYATMMREY   _ _ _ _ _ _ _ _ _

WIDEN DNLA   _ _ _ _ _ _ _ _ _ _ _

AEBRULBB   _ _ _ _ _ _ _ _

LCCKI   _ _ _ _ _

LEGAN WEOLLR   _ _ _ _ _ _ _ _ _ _ _ _

VIGTNEEA   _ _ _ _ _ _ _ _

WNLOB UTO   _ _ _ _ _ _ _ _ _

Puzzle #38
PHOTO TERMS

OBNCEU TILHG   _ _ _ _ _ _ _ _ _ _ _

HGLIT ARTP   _ _ _ _ _ _ _ _ _

OLFLAFF   _ _ _ _ _ _ _

DIENFR   _ _ _ _ _ _

SFALH NGU   _ _ _ _ _ _ _ _

OSCFU GNIR   _ _ _ _ _ _ _ _ _ _

LFUL ECAF   _ _ _ _ _ _ _ _

AEGRL GELAN   _ _ _ _ _ _ _ _ _ _

LSMI SANORA   _ _ _ _ _ _ _ _ _ _

YRAG DACR   _ _ _ _ _ _ _ _

DIGR   _ _ _ _

OGURDN SLSGA   _ _ _ _ _ _ _ _ _ _

PHOTO TERMS

LNOTA ENARG

_ _ _ _ _ _ _ _ _ _

IAREAL HOOTP

_ _ _ _ _ _ _ _ _ _ _

RHLDCAOTK

_ _ _ _ _ _ _ _ _

TORBRE ACAP

_ _ _ _ _ _ _ _ _ _

TANI ESAHK

_ _ _ _ _ _ _ _ _

KORMORAD

_ _ _ _ _ _ _ _

CNRBEKAIGT

_ _ _ _ _ _ _ _ _ _

ATXIRM

_ _ _ _ _ _

NISTOECAMPNO

_ _ _ _ _ _ _ _ _ _ _ _

EHCAB EODM

_ _ _ _ _ _ _ _ _

ORARGPM EMDO

_ _ _ _ _ _ _ _ _ _ _

ELE EMLIRL

_ _ _ _ _ _ _ _ _

PHOTO TERMS

NTCPLPIIOAA   _ _ _ _ _ _ _ _ _ _ _

IMIATGSTMAS   _ _ _ _ _ _ _ _ _ _ _

GRAHIADPM   _ _ _ _ _ _ _ _ _

AYBB TPOS   _ _ _ _ _ _ _ _ _

ICLKC OTSP   _ _ _ _ _ _ _ _ _ _

SENIONTEX   _ _ _ _ _ _ _ _ _

DBNEL   _ _ _ _ _

SELEA   _ _ _ _ _

LBBU EDOM   _ _ _ _ _ _ _ _ _

IOGZT   _ _ _ _ _

LILF HLITG   _ _ _ _ _ _ _ _ _ _

MRUEELI   _ _ _ _ _ _ _

Cryptogram
Hints

1: D=I	25: B=A
2: Z=E	26: Y=T
3: N=A	27: R=H
4: T=E	28: P=O
5: E=A	29: D=A
6: V=T	30: D=O
7: G=I	31: N=R
8: R=N	32: C=T
9: F=E	33: Y=O
10: G=E	34: H=O
11: X=T	35: H=E
12: W=A	36: J=A
13: X=T	37: A=I
14: D=A	38: G=E
15: P=O	39: Q=T
16: Z=I	40: L=E
17: B=T	41: E=T
18: R=A	42: P=A
19: Q=E	43: J=I
20: B=T	44: D=E
21: B=I	45: C=T
22: Y=A	46: K=A
23: G=N	47: C=T
24: W=O	48: X=A

49: T=A   73: G=T

50: O=T   74: S=E

51: Z=E   75: R=T

52: F=E   76: R=E

53: T=M   77: Y=T

54: U=T   78: I=T

55: T=E   79: K=A

56: E=T   80: X=A

57: P=E   81:

58: E=I   82:

59: Q=N   83:

60: F=I   84:

61: T=I   85:

62: A=O   86:

63: V=T   87:

64: M=O   88:

65: P=I   89:

66: Z=I   90:

67: Q=T   91:

68: Q=E   92:

69: Z=A   93:

70: C=T   94:

71: R=O   95:

72: H=I   96:

Cryptograms

1.

QIWDOY LDRQEKFB DB BICVKDOY NDAF

DOQFOBFNG, FCFKG ZEOXKFXQZ VA I BFRVOX.

HIKR KDSVEX

. . . .

2.

C XZCS YWRXCNRL CR WYZCR. C KPWXWBSCKPZS

NL CICSZ WE XPZ XNRH FWFZRXL NR C KZSLWRL

VNEZ XPCX SZQZCV BSZCXZS XSAXPL.   CRWR

. . . .

3.

N UXXR CYXKXUJNCY PI XFQ KYNK VXHHWFPVNKQI N

LNVK, KXWVYQI KYQ YQNJK NFR OQNBQI KYQ BPQSQJ N

VYNFUQR CQJIXF LXJ YNBPFU IQQF PK. PK PI,

PF N SXJR, QLLQVKPBQ.   PJBPFU CQFF

. . . .

4.

AX ZMT NEJKO EB YMEZECJQYMU, UED CTZ

ZE IMQJT Q PQYZDJTO SESTXZ NAZM EZMTJ

YTEYKT.   FQSTI NAKIEX

. . . .

5.

NFIK LWK EJELKDGP FEZXK EHHGNEIW EFS WDJAYK

CZYYZFRFKPP LN YKEGF OESKP ECET, LWK

IGKELZXK PHZGZL NO RNNS HWNLNRGEHWT SZKP CZLW

ZL. EYOGKS KZPKFPLEKSL

. . . .
6.

LEASL OBYYO MJYI, XQV VCBN AEDV SAZBTVJOB

MJYI; VCBN SAZBTVJOB IBIETJBO. VCBEAETB

YBZJVV

. . . .
7.

E KBWDWVJEKB GO NGXL E JLQGKL DBL ZLZWJC GO

DBL SGIGOBLH HGOB. QEJJGL NEDLD

. . . .
8.

CV AT, DWVCVBJHDWG PN CWT NPAQECHRTVQN

JTMVBRPCPVR, PR H LJHMCPVR VL H NTMVRY,

VL CWT NPBRPLPMHRMT VL HR TITRC. WTRJP

MHJCPTJ-OJTNNVR

. . . .

9.

JN MBCP ZJHVCPFL XPFUV SBBA FUBCSE, MBCPF UBV

HYBLF FUBCSE.   PBTFPV HXZX

. . . .

10.

KMNBYH MY BAMHG, XLGGSBYH M AVAGYK,

LGWGMOF CVR LBPC LGMOBKE KLIOE BF.   MYVY

. . . .

11.

BI QAPXPYDGQAZ, XAT MFGRRTMX XABIY NGI LT

G YDTGX MCLOTNX. XAT RBXXRT, ACFGI ETXGBR

NGI LTNPFT G RTBXFPXBU.   ATIDB NGDXBTD-LDTMMPI

. . . .

12.

YEBSBAZWYEC UX WR UIIPVUWSP ZPWKSUBR,

VZWNURA UX W IPVUSWSUBR.   EPRZU

KWZSUPZ-TZPXXBR

. . . .

13.

LEB RESX XDOQ GUTXBZQC; XNQL XDOQ LEB. - WDL

YDUCQI

. . . .

14.

IJOL LMATFO AT BAGK DQK IJIKTLO JG SBKDOEQK

DTH D BAGKLAIK JG KIRDQQDOOIKTL;

SMJLJFQDSMU AO D IJIKTL JG KIRDQQDOOIKTL DTH D

BAGKLAIK JG SBKDOEQK.   LJTU RKTT

. . . .

15.

PMSW TYPBPLHZTYK WMBWHD KPJH IUPPFDBHWZX, RB

RD URVW Z FRDWZDW.   ZMPM

. . . .

16.

ZD Z PACUL GNUU GXN YGAJF ZB KAJLY, Z

KACULBG BNNL GA UCV MJACBL M PMINJM.   UNKZY

XZBN

. . . .

17.

BETSXP ASDBMVUQ SQ NSTU BSABHUSXP SXBH BZU

TSBDZUX NEBU EB XSPZB EXC QBUENSXP HVUH

DHHTSUQ. CSEXU EVIMQ

. . . .

18.

PMDE PQCNZ IDVQHD WEVFDRC, T ZMRFF LQVWZ

PTBM AMQBQOCRAMZ. PMDE THRODZ IDVQHD

TERNDUWRBD, T ZMRFF ID VQEBDEB PTBM ZTFDEVD.

REZDF RNRHZ

. . . .

19.

BGXNXTIUBGZ EQUSR QVHWCRCNQSZ KCNG

UBBQUIUMOQR, AWN MXNGCMT CR KGUN CN

UBBQUIR NX AQ. EWUMQ PCOGUSR

. . . .

20.

ED VGRBRHQIVGN BGCQC IQC DR MGIWRJM BGIB PIDDRB

XC ETTLFEDIBCW. ILHLMB MIDWCQ

. . . .

21.

JS VG, KFSJSYNXKFT BZ XR XNJ SM SLZGNPXJBSR.

BJZ RSJ EHZJ XLSHJ MBRCBRY ZSVGJFBRY

BRJGNGZJBRY BR XR SNCBRXNT KWXUG BPG

MSHRC BJ FXZ GPGNTJFBRY JS CS OBJF JFG OXT TSH

ZGG JFGV.   GWWBSJJ GNOBJJ

. . . .

22.

P ABPMC HDDE ESUYXPMH PZ JBYA RUYEZ AD HDDE

GBDADHSYGBZ.   JYQMU XPRRUS

. . . .

23.

TFEJEKCPTFW AL P HPDEC MECQS AG SZTOPAGAGK

HPG JE HPG.   SNXPCN LJSAQFSG

. . . .

24.

UFA SMLUIBA UFJU HWI UWWP TMUF HWIB LJGABJ

MR UFA MGJZMOJUMWO HWI TJOU UW LBAJUA TMUF

BAJNMUH.   RLWUU NWBAOKW

. . . .

25.

WRXAX BAX BQJBTK WJF UXFUQX OE XMXAT

UOSWLAX: WRX URFWFYABURXA BEP WRX

MOXJXA.   BEKXQ BPBNK

. . . .

26.

X LSTYTBQXLS KU X UVWQVY XHTNY X UVWQVY. YSV

FTQV KY YVOOU CTN YSV OVUU CTN JATD.   PKXAV

XQHNU

. . . .

27.

CRQP JKL MRKIKDOWMR W AWGQ . . .JKL

MRKIKDOWMR IRQ VKLZ EQRTPU TI.   HQWP-ZLG

DKUWOU

. . . .

28.

LV RPA TSMB BP QJ S QJBBJF KGPBPIFSKGJF,

XBSMY LM VFPMB PV HPFJ LMBJFJXBLMI XBAVV.   NLH

FLDGSFYXPM

. . . .

29.

TF VCK YFYG DPY KV TVPY ZWDK GSVEZG VK D

XPYINTNKDPF GYDPSW, ZWY SDTYPDG YFY TDF

YKZNPYIF SWDKUY TF NQYD.   YQCDPQ CYGZVK

. . . .

30.

NPY HWLYIW ZA WF YOHRAY ND QY ADLYXTWHY SDR

DNPYIJZAY CDFN QYTDFB. ZN BZGYA LY QDNP W

XDZFN DV HDFFYHNZDF WFC W XDZFN DV AYXWIWNZDF.

ARAWF LYZAYTWA

. . . .

31.

LVWN XMVAVCNHXML JD H NPUVNQ VB LVWN FJIJKC,

BVN HKLVKP OMV NPHFFL DPPD.   XHWF DANHKQ

. . . .

32.

L RDIC CUAPC FDURP. L CUAPC QLXCAUMP.

KLOOMP QMUMPP

. . . .

33.

NYZ TYQD DXGO X MRYDYBCXMR, NYZ EXGO

WD.　XQAOI XTXEA

. . . .

34.

DHJG LKGPZ 10,000 CXHZHTGWCXP WGI DHJG

MHGPZ.　XIVGK AWGZKIG-YGIPPHV

. . . .

35.

NLEH LW NLAH J KJVHTJ. IPWZ EUKPW UF DOJZW

LVCUTZJFZ JFX KJCZPTH ZOH MUUX ZLVHW, XHQHNUC

ETUV ZOH FHMJZLQHW JFX LE ZOLFMW XUFZ DUTA

UPZ, IPWZ ZJAH JFUZOHT WOUZ.　JFUF

. . . .

36.

OT AYELOJEZ NQJY LP EQ EIT EQ OJFZ EKZ

QICLHJIT YQQF ZGEIJQICLHJIT　OJIELH

UJII

. . . .

37.

GLYJYRXBGLS AT JLH XHUYXMADR YK

TJXBDRHDHTT BDM PHBWJS QAJL PHRWAIADR

GXHUATAYD. THPBTJABD TVHH

. . . .
38.

RGZNAU YZM RG CGGM VM ZPP AJVMOC, CGGVMO ZMF

YLWKLCVMO AJG RGZNAU VC HJZA CGKZQZAGC AJG

CMZKCJLA DQLW AJG KJLALOQZKJ. WZAA JZQFU

. . . .
39.

QXV PNRVMN WVVW RKMV QXNB QXV VIV, WK FXI

BKQ RNEV TWV KH OQ? VJFNMJ FVWQKB

. . . .
40.

SELJL YB TZL SEYZO SEL WETSTOJUWE KHBS

DTZSUYZ SEL EHKUZYSA TC SEL KTKLZS. JTMLJS

CJUZG

. . . .

41.

STA CSAKTE KESN KAAOTV. STA CSAKTE KESN

MQDJOTV. OE CSAKTE ELQT SMM DTC ELQT ST. OEK ST

DHH EBA EOJA.   DTTOA HAOGSXOER

. . . .
42.

KL HDTO DI IRPSON YL VRO ZCJOUV UOON VW QPUNOC

PUN WYIOCBO, PUN KL EPKOCP DI KL SPIISWCV.

IVOBO KEEZCCL

. . . .
43.

UAGI J OAQYQRTCOA, UACY JB TGCSSE XQJIR JP

PGGFJIR CIPUGTP YQ YAJIRP.   UEII DLSSQZF

. . . .
44.

FD BVD CBGNPJ IMHRHJVBIMZ RH

WPADVZRBPA FMBR HWV TNQDZ CDBP RH WZ.

VBTIM MBRRDVZTDL

. . . .

45.

G QMKCKGWC WN UMC LGFZ WU CIZ YGLZKG XAC MU

ZWCIZK NWFZ MH WC.   ZFTGKF NCZWYIZU

. . . .

46.

DJQ WKRQVK XT KA XATDVHRQAD DJKD

DQKWJQT IQGINQ JGE DG TQQ EXDJGHD K WKRQVK.

CGVGDJQK NKAMQ

. . . .

47.

XCN ZRD CKXRT CZ ELVD L UXHCQID ZG JKLC L

UDINZR BZZVN BXVD, XCN LRZCKDI CKXRT CZ ELVD L

UZICILXC ZG JKZ CKDP LID.   ULQB HLUZRXTIZ

. . . .

48.

YMCB SBUCURKXSBI X VAY OXVRPXRA BXE JAAV

TKAXCAW. YA TXV OUUN XC XV MDSKAEEMUV XE OUVR

XE YA YMEB, YA TXV WAOLA MVCU MC XVW, EU

CU ESAXN, KAVAY SXEC AHSAKMAVTAE XC YMOO. -

XVUV

. . . .

49.

RJ MEZT CI T KCCE NMXDWHZ ML CSZ DYTDL

MS ICXWL TSE CI T ITRCWL NZHLCS. TSEJ

VTHYCO

. . . .
50.

PIGO H VHTY GJRCO WIRORQXGWIE HE OIGO

OIYZ UGWOCXY G FRFYDO OIGOE QRDY SRXYBYX,

HFWREEHJVY OR XYWXRLCUY. TGXV

VGQYXSYVL

. . . .
51.

WGMRMLJEWGA UT E BZEVT KA CGUIG CZ DZEJV RM

TZZ RGZ MJSUVEJA. SEYUS KEUDZA

. . . .
52.

LUVPLGGD, ZX MNV LGG VSLV ZMVFIFAVFY ZM VSF

APKQFUV NW RSNVNCILRSD. NMUF VSF RZUVPIF ZA ZM

VSF KNT, ZX MNV LGG VSLV ZMVFIFAVFY ZM JSLV

SLRRFMA MFTV. SPMVFIA, LWVFI LGG, LIFMV UNNOA.

 SFMIZ ULIVZFI-KIFAANM

. . . .

53.

EYSG BSFBPS RML TS EYRO SJAHBTSGO H AMS H

OSPP OYST TC SCSM.   RGFG

. . . .

54.

NIIB JXY UKHXB LFVISF ICFXHXE UKF QKPUUFS.

UKF KFJSU JXY DHXY JSF UKF USPF NFXQ IV UKF

OJDFSJ.   MIPQPV BJSQK

. . . .

55.

FMVT MG NII GAICN NI GTT GIWTIST RIL FIYT MS

KBH FMXANMSX - BSIS

. . . .

56.

SZRBE CYXEXSZBCYJ FU BIXLE PRCEY XV

VRRHFGS, GXE PRCEY XV VFRHP.   CRERZ BPBQU

. . . .

57.

OG OZ RWSP ORIWSGYFG GW XJOXA BOGN IPWIJP GNYF

GW XJOXA GNP ZNDGGPS.   YJKSPE POZPFZGYPEG

. . . .
58.

HTY XTWNY JWEOH WA HUFEOB JEKHMVYP EP PW

HTUH SWM ZWOH TUGY HW YCJNUEO HTEOBP XEHT

XWVZP.   YNNEWHH YVXEHH

. . . .
59.

RD TAE KSS KAOSLYRQP LYCL OAMSK TAE, CQJ

LYSQ KQCZ RL, TAE VSSZ C OAOSQL.   NRQJC

OGGCILQST

. . . .
60.

F QFNB CBIC ITT PS VICWGHN KIRVFSFLHVLH,

CBH HKPCFPV PS CBH TIVZ, CBH TFJFVR HVHGRE

PS OTILH LPWTZ MH OBPCPRGIOBHZ.   IVVFH

THFMPJFCA

. . . .

61.

BRVSVDMXBR: X BTHSKMC BXTZSCW JN SRC PKZ
GTSRVKS TZPSMKHSTVZ TZ XMS. XFJMVPC JTCMHC

. . . .

62.

SEAVAYCXSEJ GI VEP IVACJ G BXGO VA SMV GKVA
TACQI. QPIVGK ISXCUI

. . . .

63.

K QHJO VBO IOHIQO K IBHVHTEPIB. K NOPZ,
VBOCEO NC MEKOZFY. KJO ZOJOE NOV NHYV HM VBON
HE K FHZV UZHL VBON PV PQQ, COV VBEHSTB NC
KNPTOY K QKJO LKVB VBON. XESAO TKQFOZ

. . . .

64.

MJGP EMC YPBZJ KM GBZP, EMC GBJ ZPGMZV SUBIPN
LSKW EMCZ USJV MZ MJ XSYU. KWPZP SN JM
VSXXPZPJGP QPKLPPJ KWP KLM. BJMJ

. . . .

65.

P AZYRRW LZRPZOZ XQZAZ YAZ XQPTKF TILIJW

MINRJ FZZ PE P JPJTX SQIXIKAYSQ XQZD.   JPYTZ

YALNF

. . . .

66.

MIEBECLUMIH IUG SE LWAXG, ZB ZG SEB U

GMELB. ZB ZG BIX LXGWAB YIZRI REWSBG, SE JUBBXL

IEY ZB ZG URIZXNXO.   KZAA KLUSOB

. . . .

67.

CYR NYUQ QFTL F SJYQYBIFSJ. CYR FKT

ZRGLQDC QY EYIIYH GQ.   FUYU

. . . .

68.

WYXGXTIRWYP BD GIFGY. GYQ OBUQHR BD GIFGY

GMQUGP-LXFI GBHQD WQI DQOXUN.   SQRU-VFO

TXNRIN

. . . .

69.

H CVBVU SZBV MZAVC Z EHKMQUV HBV HCMVCGVG.

MSVRUV ZFIZRJ LVMMVU TU ITUJV. GHZCV ZULQJ

. . . .

70.

CAS USJWCLPS LV CAS SNMLPWDSUC YT CAS

GYBEYVSZV VGYZS WUF CAS EZLUC, CAS ESZTYZBWUGS.

 WUVSD WFWBV

. . . .

71.

COB JULBMU LUIBV ERZ KRMNBC ERZMB COBMB.

XCV HRC FXIB ERZ UMB OXQXHN YZC ERZ KRMNBC,

ERZ UMB TZVC FRRIXHN VR LZJO. UHHXB FBXYRWXCD

. . . .

72.

NYYNOAHLRRZ FULA CUTATMGLCUZ HY HY RHPN

RHA DC. YLE LQNRR

. . . .

73.

GIM KMBG GILYP DKCAG D OLEGAHM LB GIDG LG

YMFMH EIDYPMB, MFMY JIMY GIM OMCOWM LY LG

XC.   DYXV JDHICW

. . . .

74.

IKMAMNEZIKH UO ZP ZWOASES ZPF XTZDUPN

IMSAEH MG AKS ESZT.   ZPOST ZFZJO

. . . .

75.

PT RJF XJBRBVQOXJFQ PD PLRFQFDRFN PL RJF

XFBXUF PL TQBLR BT JPD UFLD, OLN PT JF PD

WBHXODDPBLORF, PRD OUQFONA O UBR. RJF

PLDRQIHFLR PD LBR RJF WOHFQO CIR RJF

XJBRBVQOXJFQ.   FKF OQLBUN

. . . .

76.

EGG ULKHKONEULA ENR ESSZNEHR. JKJR KP HLRF

BA HLR HNZHL.   NBSLENV ECRVKJ

. . . .

77.

T YGOUZ YGTY BKX MAA OU CB NOJYXWAM OM YGTY O

QTM UKY TVWTOS YK VTHH OU HKLA QOYG YGAMA

NAKNHA.   TUUOA HAOEKLOYF

. . . .

78.

XH LJEIEWNMLJF, IJONO XC M NOMTXIF CE CDUITO

IJMI XI UOBEKOC KENO NOMT IJMH NOMTXIF.

MTYNOQ CIXOWTXIS

. . . .

79.

CWSDSXMKCWU DKARL KI OILDKID SFD SE DOBR,

KQDRMOIX QOER VU WSQPOIX OD LDOQQ.

PSMSDWRK QKIXR

. . . .

80.

IPJN SZIUIQWXSZ RZXU NIC JILG. UHB RXJTGW

. . . .

Photography #1 - Solution

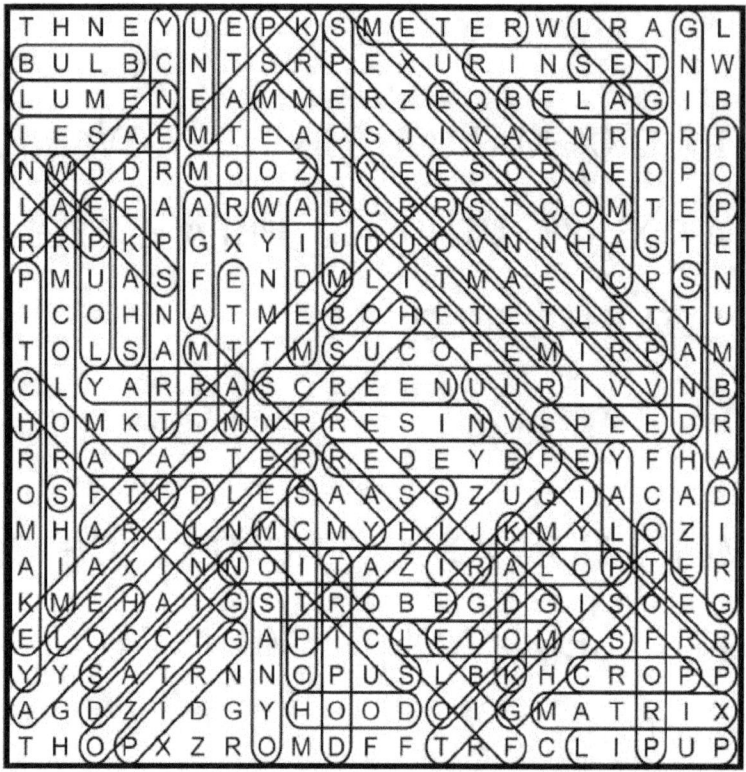

Photography #2 - Solution

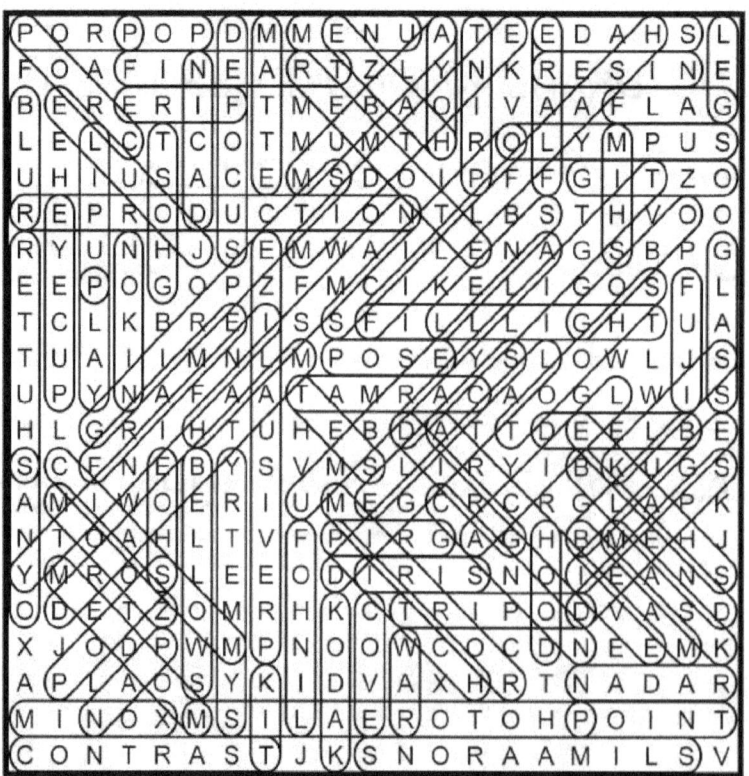

Photography #3 - Solution

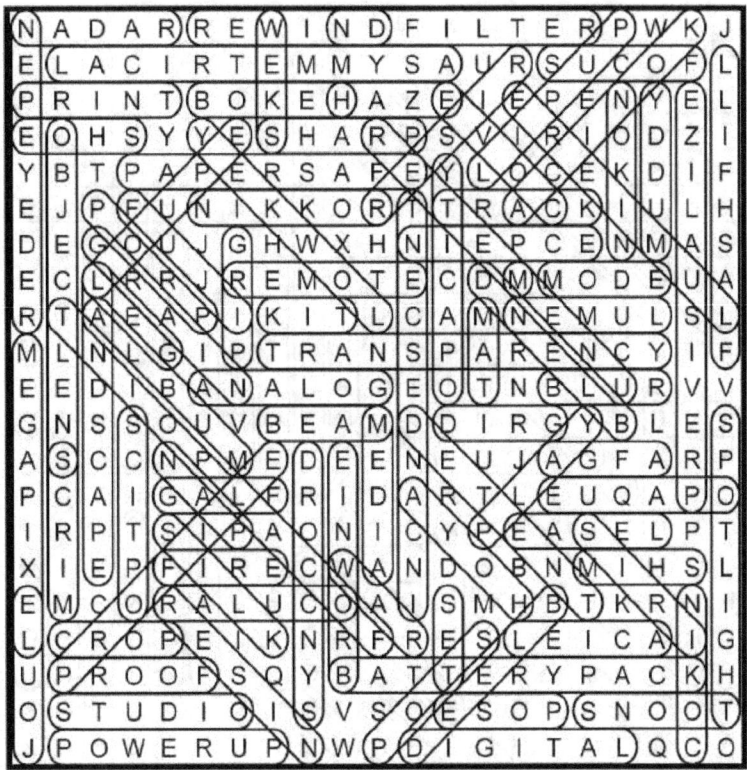

Photography #4 - Solution

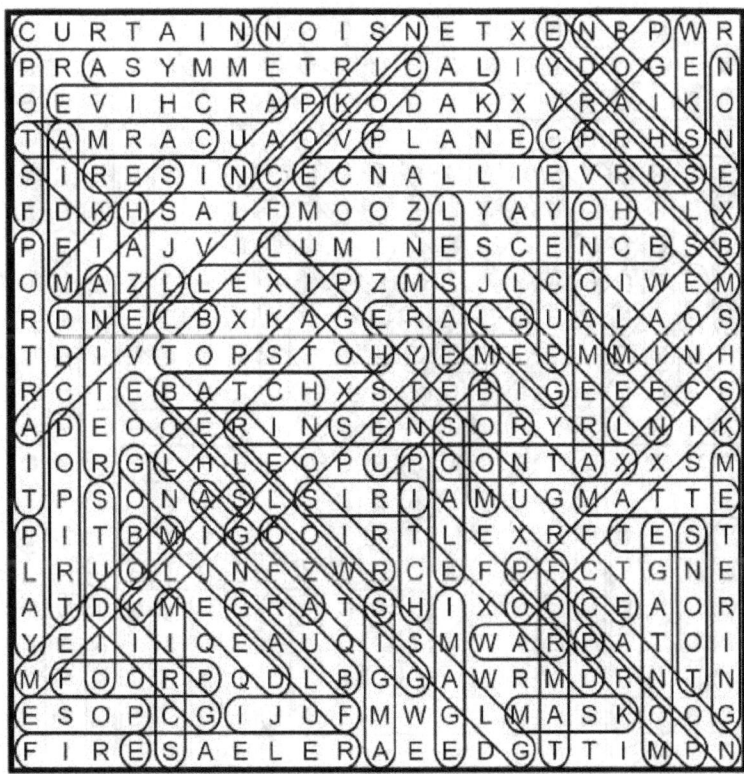

Photography #5 - Solution

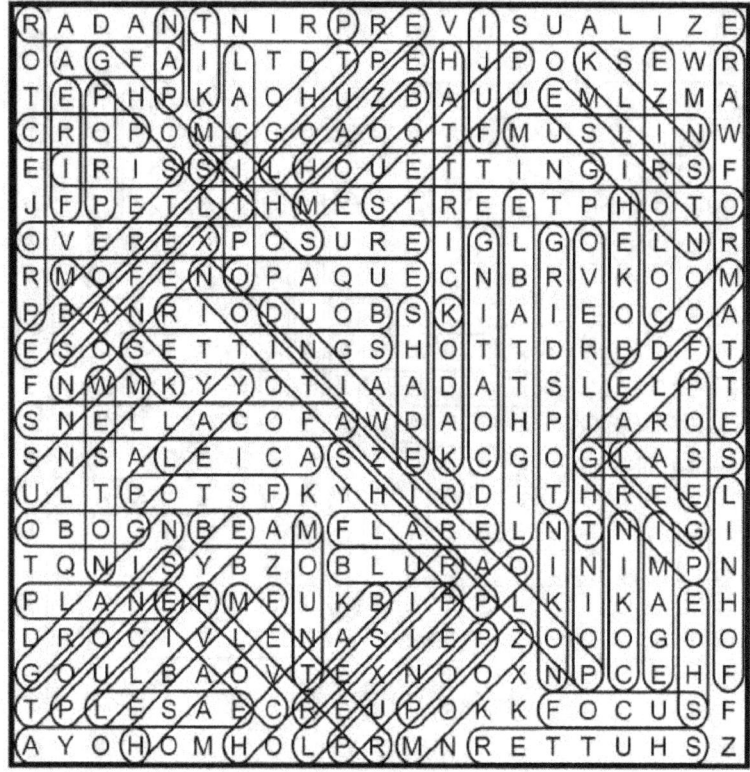

Photography #6 - Solution

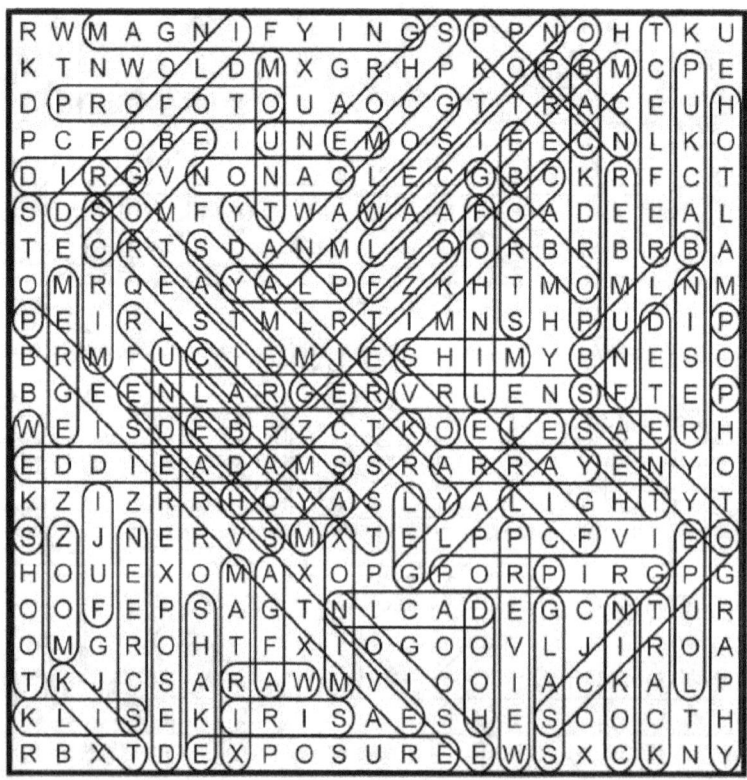

Photography #7 - Solution

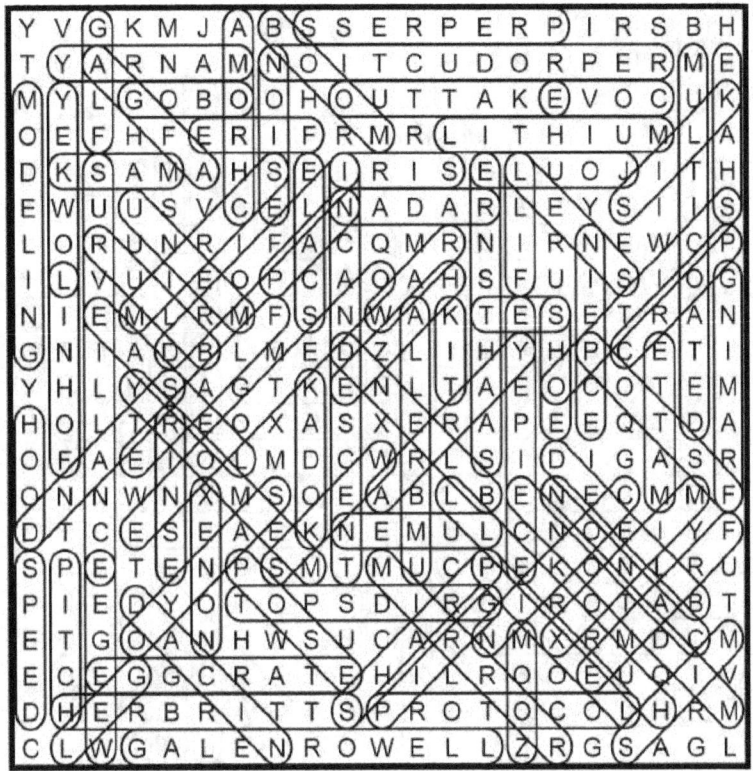

Photography #8 - Solution

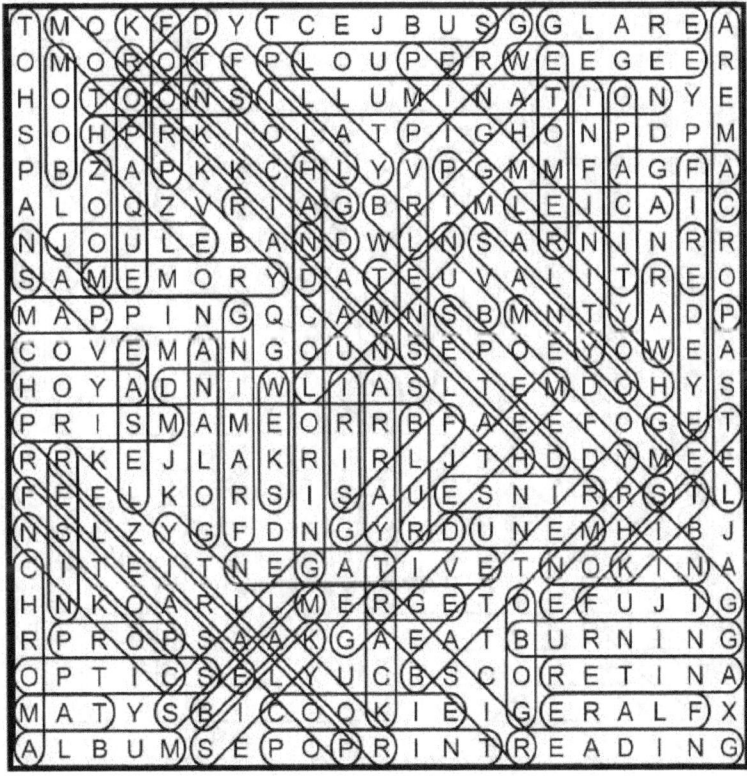

Photography #9 - Solution

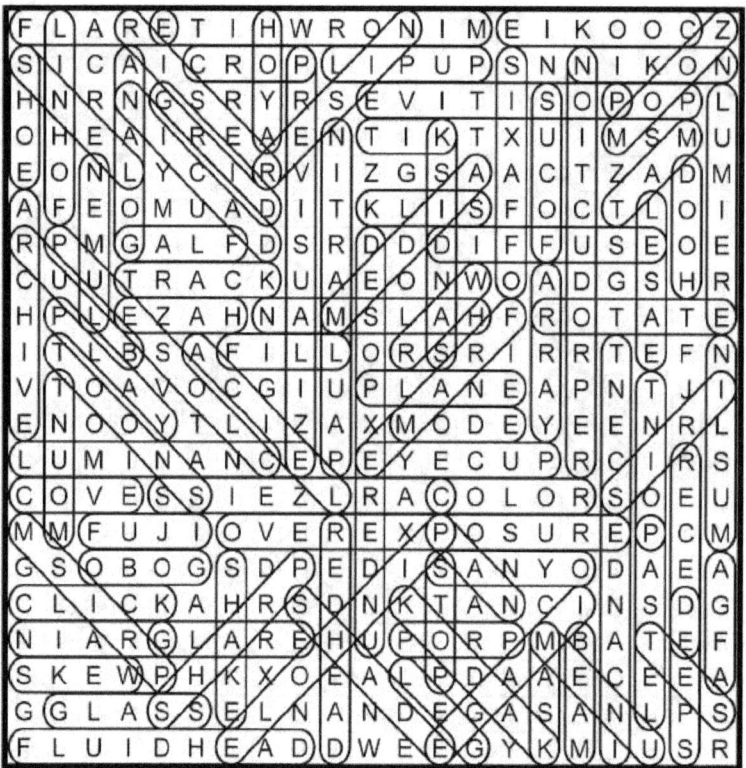

Photography #10 - Solution

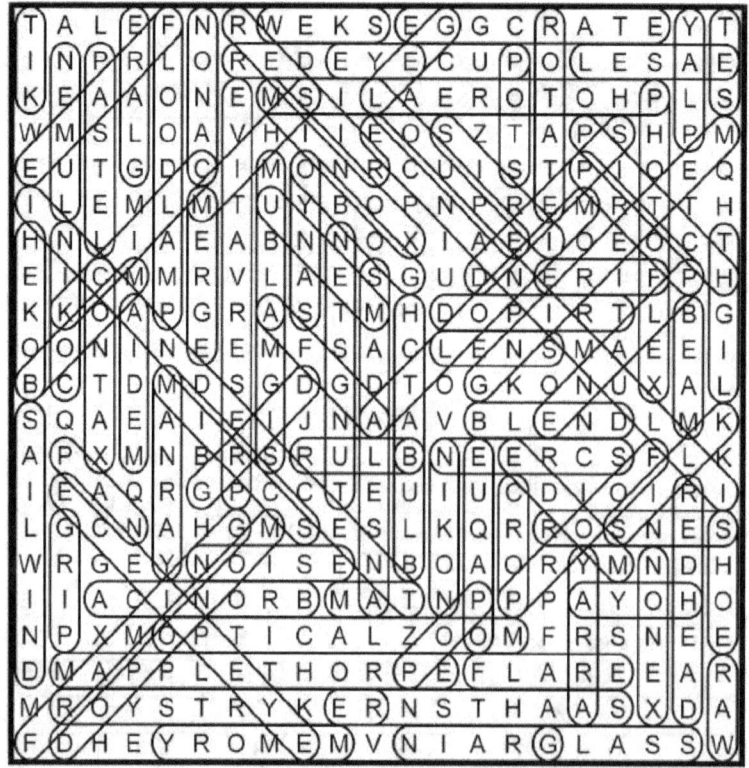

Photography #11 - Solution

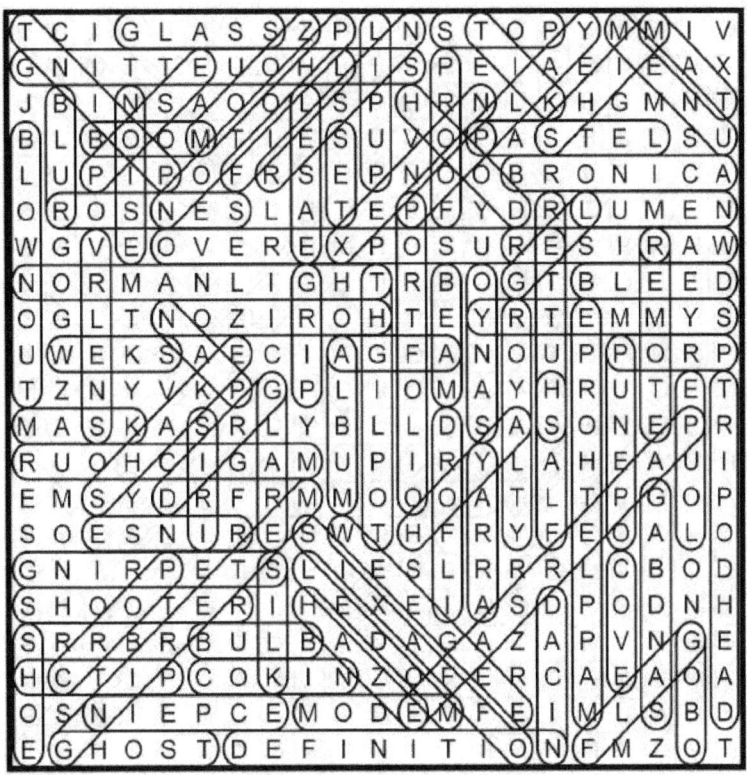

Photography #12 - Solution

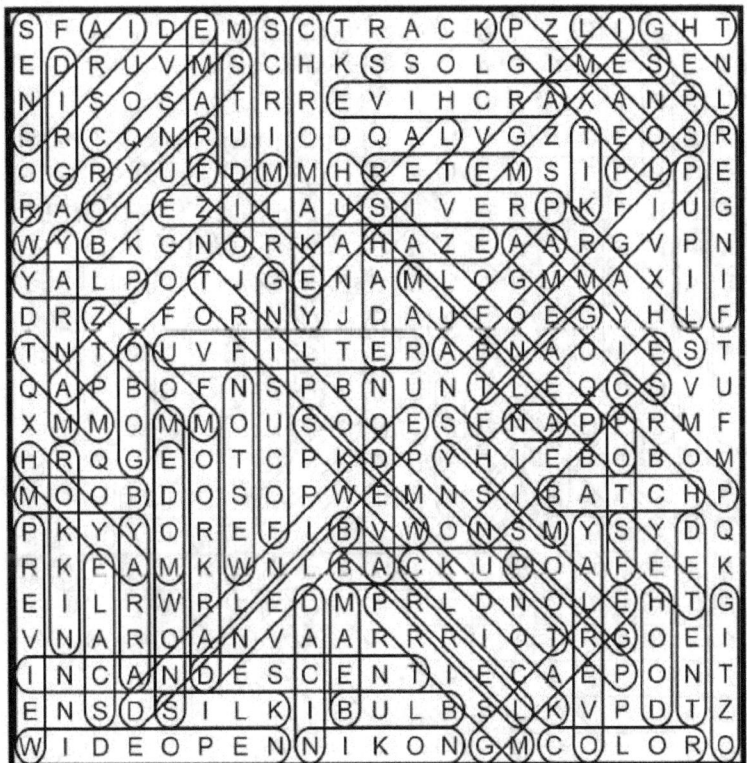

Photography #13 - Solution

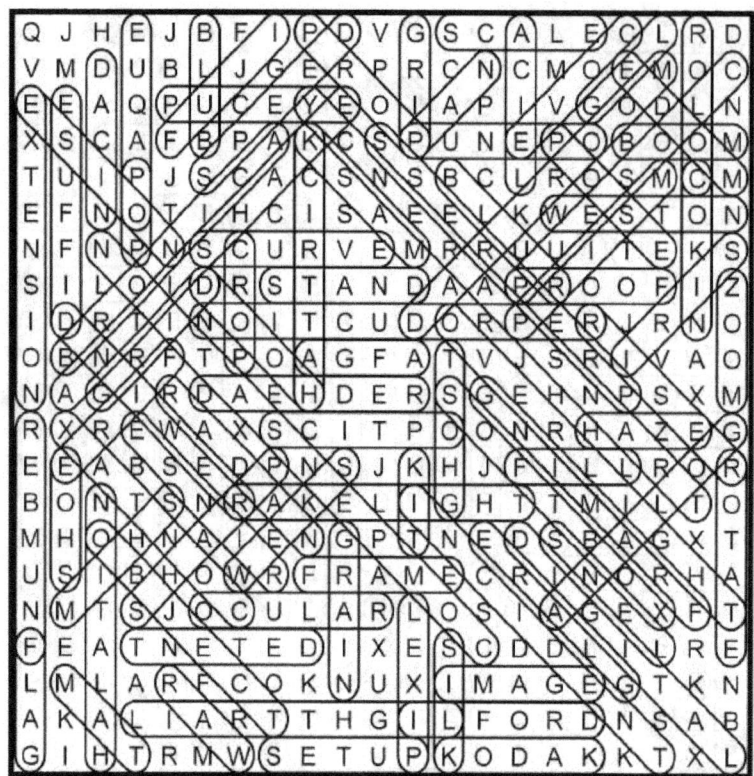

Photography #14 - Solution

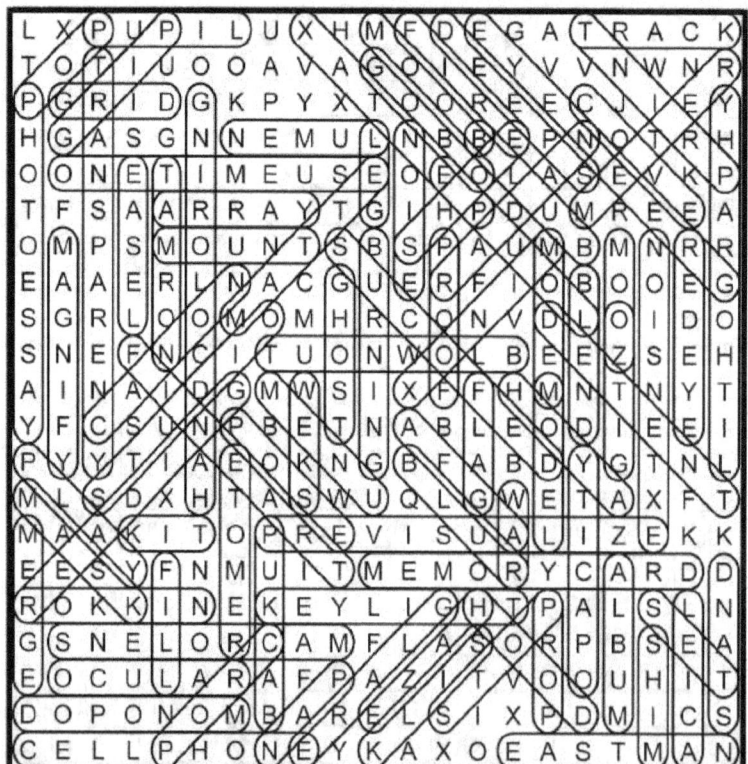

Photography #15 - Solution

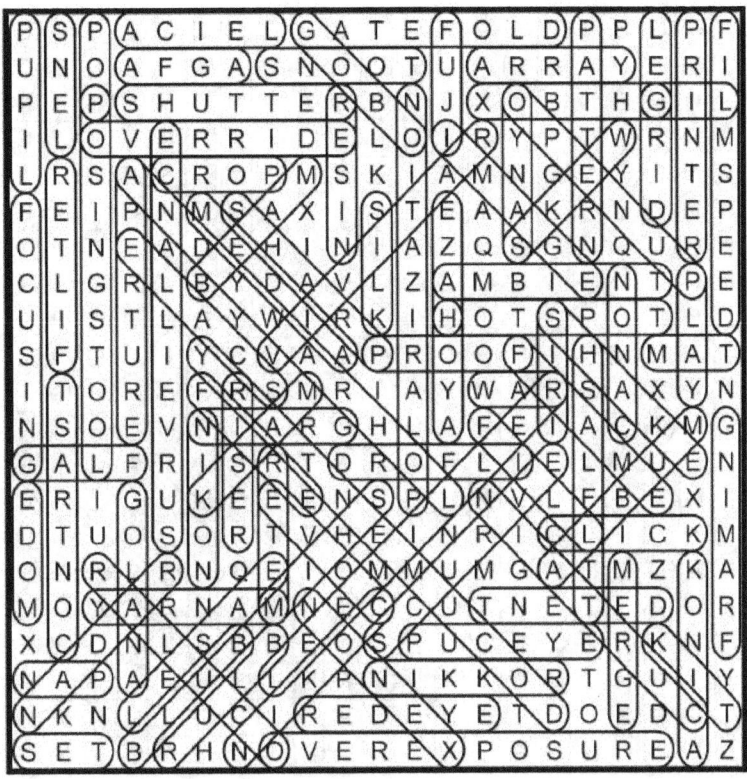

Photography #16 - Solution

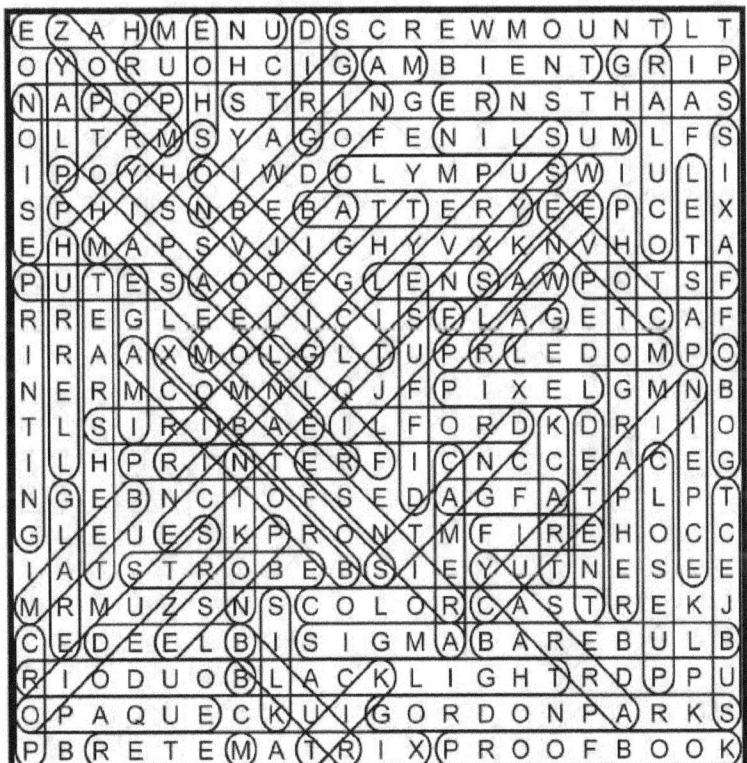

Photography #17 - Solution

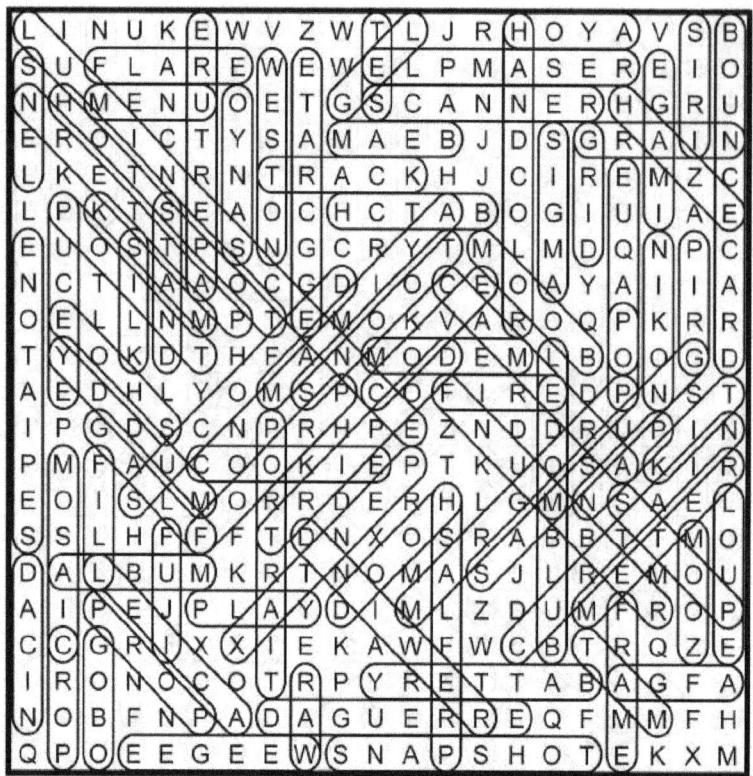

Photography #18 - Solution

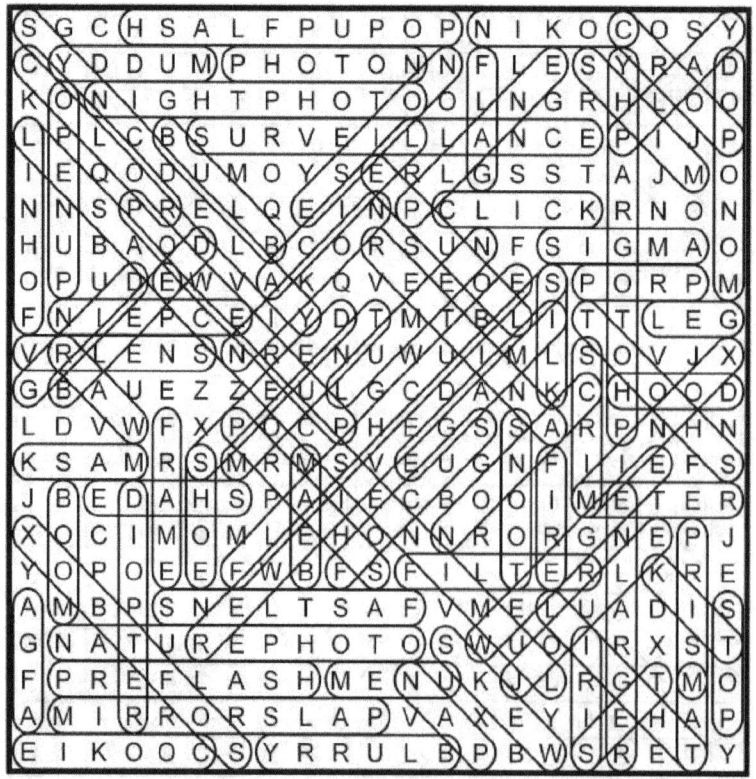

Photography #19 - Solution

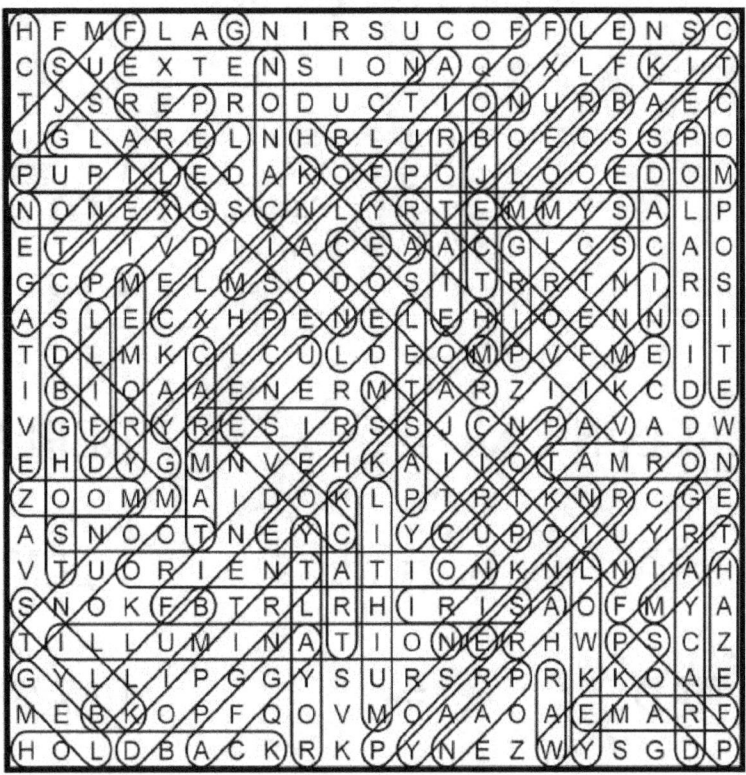

Photography #20 - Solution

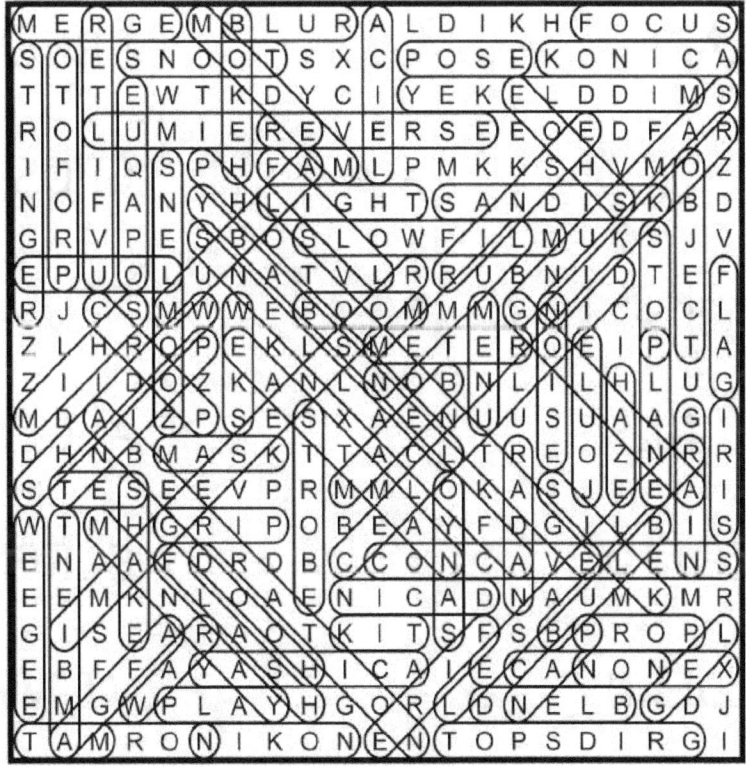

PHOTO TERMS

PEULO	=	LOUPE
SIFUERDF	=	DIFFUSER
FEETRLACECN	=	REFLECTANCE
IFLM FSEA	=	FILM SAFE
AHFSL RADC	=	FLASH CARD
CLFOA LPEAN	=	FOCAL PLANE
NLCEEEARF	=	FREELANCE
HGSOT	=	GHOST
OSSRC IHGLT	=	CROSS LIGHT
OAACFL NLSE	=	AFOCAL LENS
ASENSIETEDT	=	EISENSTAEDT
RVEFIIDEWN	=	VIEWFINDER

PHOTO TERMS

MAASENT	=	EASTMAN
URNGIBN	=	BURNING
WLO TCNOTSAR	=	LOW CONTRAST
MLIF DSEPE	=	FILM SPEED
LASFH UECB	=	FLASH CUBE
LFCOA OIPTN	=	FOCAL POINT
EREEFZ OFCSU	=	FREEZE FOCUS
NSEL AREFL	=	LENS FLARE
OLOP HGITL	=	LOOP LIGHT
EETDRAUATS	=	DESATURATE
TBINMEA	=	AMBIENT
ATILYDHG	=	DAYLIGHT

PHOTO TERMS

UNLLNAIIIOTM	=	ILLUMINATION
FLUETYBTR	=	BUTTERFLY
TSAF ELNS	=	FAST LENS
EFRIGN	=	FINGER
CRONBAI	=	BRONICA
OUFCS TFSIH	=	FOCUS SHIFT
LLFU EGNLTH	=	FULL LENGTH
LGSAS	=	GLASS
CTENIHORGU	=	RETOUCHING
REGNE EEY	=	GREEN EYE
PRIG	=	GRIP
IRAH IHTGL	=	HAIR LIGHT

PHOTO TERMS

NAIRBTRAEO	=	ABERRATION
ROLOC ACTS	=	COLOR CAST
LNTAGEMENER	=	ENLARGEMENT
ILBL NARBDT	=	BILL BRANDT
LUDLLOECI	=	CELLULOID
TSTAOROOPH	=	ASTROPHOTO
DAYN HLROWA	=	ANDY WARHOL
EFLTIR	=	FILTER
RNBA ROSOD	=	BARN DOORS
CBTAH	=	BATCH
OOWLRPE	=	LOWEPRO
IFRLEPO	=	PROFILE

PHOTO TERMS

EEY PCU	=	EYE CUP
ELSN LENMETE	=	LENS ELEMENT
HGLTI ETNT	=	LIGHT TENT
OCOLR LEWHE	=	COLOR WHEEL
MTPOOIECS	=	COMPOSITE
AOEPRLHPTEMP	=	MAPPLETHORPE
NAVOCEC ENSL	=	CONCAVE LENS
OMZO	=	ZOOM
RNOMI EHWIT	=	MINOR WHITE
UNEILMCNA	=	LUMINANCE
KBCAL ACRD	=	BLACK CARD
LEBU ECNESR	=	BLUE SCREEN

PHOTO TERMS

TPEERUAR	=	APERTURE
ECVO	=	COVE
ORCMA EDOM	=	MACRO MODE
ITGILHNG	=	LIGHTING
LBSELOW	=	BELLOWS
IGHTL BAETL	=	LIGHT TABLE
RCOP	=	CROP
PCEINE	=	NIEPCE
IOKCN	=	COKIN
ECMAAR KSHEA	=	CAMERA SHAKE
LFIL	=	FILL
LFEAR	=	FLARE

PHOTO TERMS

NNOEX	=	XENON
TDMILAMIUE	=	MULTIMEDIA
FOF ISXA	=	OFF AXIS
IEPSPEOSMRU	=	SUPERIMPOSE
GTHAPORPOH	=	PHOTOGRAPH
IPHCT	=	PITCH
OTAIIZNOLAPR	=	POLARIZATION
FASELHPR	=	PREFLASH
ROOOPFT	=	PROFOTO
ECIUNARLEVLS	=	SURVEILLANCE
YOIRCTPRCIE	=	RECIPROCITY
EMETOR	=	REMOTE

PHOTO TERMS

LLIF AFLSH	=	FILL FLASH
EMLUN	=	LUMEN
ALOCF NRGEA	=	FOCAL RANGE
RACOM SNEL	=	MACRO LENS
LAXEPIMGE	=	MEGAPIXEL
ILSLT OPTOH	=	STILL PHOTO
EUDN OTHOP	=	NUDE PHOTO
MNPOAARA	=	PANORAMA
LHDOPOOTOF	=	PHOTOFLOOD
MIGTPNE	=	PIGMENT
YLAP	=	PLAY
WRPOE PU	=	POWER UP

PHOTO TERMS

NOCAN = CANON

EVTSPIIO = POSITIVE

AFST LFMI = FAST FILM

NEFI IGARN = FINE GRAIN

SHALF ERETM = FLASH METER

SFUCO KOLC = FOCUS LOCK

LULF AFEMR = FULL FRAME

ELRAG NZEO = GLARE ZONE

RUYTRAILGAN = GRANULARITY

CELGRYAAS = GRAYSCALE

RDSGIPTO = GRIDSPOT

DEUGI MNBREU = GUIDE NUMBER

PHOTO TERMS

LNOATIAH	=	HALATION
RDHA GHTLI	=	HARD LIGHT
ZHAE ELRITF	=	HAZE FILTER
RAHOSGTMI	=	HISTOGRAM
DOOH	=	HOOD
OTH OTPS	=	HOT SPOT
TILOMNA	=	MINOLTA
YECUHPFORS	=	HYPERFOCUS
MIEAG RAEA	=	IMAGE AREA
ERRLULH	=	HURRELL
TNSNIIETY	=	INTENSITY
LUJEO	=	JOULE

PHOTO TERMS

GTINEHRSSB = BRIGHTNESS

DN TLRIEF = ND FILTER

NGTRFEHIAE = FEATHERING

EFIR = FIRE

SFAHL WADOHS = FLASH SHADOW

EBWNORI = BROWNIE

LLFU ESCAL = FULL SCALE

SYLOSG = GLOSSY

IGNRA = GRAIN

TTIGENEV = VIGNETTE

MECIARLSYTMA = ASYMMETRICAL

EBYATTR = BATTERY

PHOTO TERMS

RNECTOERV	=	CONVERTER
CNIFOSUG	=	FOCUSING
IORDNTSOTI	=	DISTORTION
XOCNVE NESL	=	CONVEX LENS
OEKOIC	=	COOKIE
OLCO SOOLCR	=	COOL COLORS
KBGHCLATI	=	BACKLIGHT
RTMGNIEE	=	METERING
VENDAO	=	AVEDON
TLHGI REEMT	=	LIGHT METER
HALFS NSCY	=	FLASH SYNC
MECARA	=	CAMERA

PHOTO TERMS

SAOTCRNT	=	CONTRAST
MEACAR HONEP	=	CAMERA PHONE
NKCAOI	=	KONICA
NWYN LLKOCUB	=	WYNN BULLOCK
TLIODGFLHO	=	FLOODLIGHT
OGLYHTRAIHP	=	LITHOGRAPHY
ZSEFISNZU	=	FUZZINESS
OBGO	=	GOBO
TEHURST	=	SHUTTER
DALIBR OPTHO	=	BRIDAL PHOTO
LHFAS ENGAR	=	FLASH RANGE
GFO RTFLIE	=	FOG FILTER

PHOTO TERMS

NMA AYR	=	MAN RAY
AEHZ	=	HAZE
IHLGGTIHH	=	HIGHLIGHT
BOMCEYONH	=	HONEYCOMB
IRONHOZ	=	HORIZON
OTH TGIHL	=	HOT LIGHT
NUNGIHT	=	HUNTING
EGIAM	=	IMAGE
RSETN AHSA	=	ERNST HAAS
ELACI	=	LEICA
SIIR	=	IRIS
YKE TLGIH	=	KEY LIGHT

PHOTO TERMS

OLDFIR	=	ILFORD
LLCE NOEHP	=	CELL PHONE
RFIUGE DUSTY	=	FIGURE STUDY
OLGN SFCOU	=	LONG FOCUS
IFDLU EADH	=	FLUID HEAD
ONTEHOFERSR	=	FORESHORTEN
EAFGRFS AETP	=	GAFFERS TAPE
ELGDON ROHU	=	GOLDEN HOUR
NTHSECIE	=	STEICHEN
ILGHT VLLEE	=	LIGHT LEVEL
THLGI EALNP	=	LIGHT PANEL
IOLTSUHETE	=	SILHOUETTE

PHOTO TERMS

NMRECAOTYUD	=	DOCUMENTARY
ADRAN	=	NADAR
USDOEFC	=	DEFOCUS
YBAB HTOSPO	=	BABY PHOTOS
IDEAN SUABR	=	DIANE ARBUS
GMAIE	=	IMAGE
EDEBL	=	BLEED
OOMB	=	BOOM
OXTANC	=	CONTAX
EIIDFNOTNI	=	DEFINITION
AITRBLNUC	=	LUBRICANT
GAFL	=	FLAG

PHOTO TERMS

EUSTRTH	=	SHUTTER
OHAYRKEMC	=	CHROMAKEY
YRO YKRETRS	=	ROY STRYKER
GADCUBNORK	=	BACKGROUND
PESATC IROTA	=	ASPECT RATIO
GEAIM ROSNSE	=	IMAGE SENSOR
LNIKEV PETM	=	KELVIN TEMP
ECCNTESNANDI	=	INCANDESCENT
GILHT ELAK	=	LIGHT LEAK
LEMIDD AYRG	=	MIDDLE GRAY
IROEDTP	=	DIOPTER
LSEAV NTIU	=	SLAVE UNIT

PHOTO TERMS

OACNBIIRTLA = CALIBRATION

IVEW ERMACA = VIEW CAMERA

DBAOR IGTLH = BROAD LIGHT

REMTE = METER

UBLB = BULB

TAIGCTLHHC = CATCHLIGHT

THO ESHO = HOT SHOE

NLES PEDES = LENS SPEED

NFITYNII = INFINITY

AOYH = HOYA

ROOGND ARKSP = GORDON PARKS

TGLHI XBO = LIGHT BOX

PHOTO TERMS

THWAEM RBAYD	=	MATHEW BRADY
OGGDIND	=	DODGING
AACMRE SFHAL	=	CAMERA FLASH
LETFRI AKCP	=	FILTER PACK
SAHLF ILFL	=	FLASH FILL
CUIEEECNLSNM	=	LUMINESCENCE
RNLEFSE SLNE	=	FRESNEL LENS
RGELA	=	GLARE
TDERAPA	=	ADAPTER
TRSETUH RDAG	=	SHUTTER DRAG
NETETD	=	DETENT
UAPL RDSTAN	=	PAUL STRAND

PHOTO TERMS

EECTAAT LMFI   =   ACETATE FILM

SENL   =   LENS

MZOO SNLE   =   ZOOM LENS

OAANLG   =   ANALOG

ELFTRI   =   FILTER

RRYAA   =   ARRAY

SOTUCFOUA   =   AUTOFOCUS

SHBGINERST   =   BRIGHTNESS

EHRB ISTRT   =   HERB RITTS

MHSALNA   =   HALSMAN

LKBAC IHTLG   =   BLACK LIGHT

IMTUHLI   =   LITHIUM

PHOTO TERMS

BNAESBLY	=	LENSBABY
PEDRUESONEX	=	UNDEREXPOSE
IHGTL RUESOC	=	LIGHT SOURCE
CEEIEPEY	=	EYEPIECE
EEONEVGNCCR	=	CONVERGENCE
CASBCKTRETA	=	BACKSCATTER
OPCY NDTAS	=	COPY STAND
GRADFEINNRE	=	RANGEFINDER
CPDASLAEN	=	LANDSCAPE
ELVPEEDOR	=	DEVELOPER
GHHI YKE	=	HIGH KEY
DHEDHLAN	=	HANDHELD

PHOTO TERMS

OYPC NLSE	=	COPY LENS
UCSFO CLKO	=	FOCUS LOCK
RGYCIOHPT	=	COPYRIGHT
AENOFRITRC	=	REFRACTION
RLAC ISZSE	=	CARL ZEISS
NIFE TAR	=	FINE ART
ROUEPXSE	=	EXPOSURE
HITGL	=	LIGHT
ACBK PU	=	BACK UP
MBEA	=	BEAM
LAWREK VASEN	=	WALKER EVANS
AMREAC YODB	=	CAMERA BODY

PHOTO TERMS

YCSCSOAER = ACCESSORY

OOLCR = COLOR

BALMU = ALBUM

GONTCAI = COATING

REUADERG = DAGUERRE

TRTPAIRO = PORTRAIT

NTHCTMTEAA = ATTACHMENT

LHSFA = FLASH

XPNEDOUDSEER = UNDEREXPOSED

ABTYETR PGIR = BATTERY GRIP

FGAA = AGFA

TGESZITLI = STIEGLITZ

PHOTO TERMS

OMSTOPNCIIO	=	COMPOSITION
LAPDRWENECO	=	CANDLEPOWER
HNILFO	=	LINHOF
URYBLR	=	BLURRY
UORRODFENG	=	FOREGROUND
IXEDF SUFCO	=	FIXED FOCUS
TFOLGEAD	=	GATEFOLD
AUMALN DMOE	=	MANUAL MODE
RPTINGNI	=	PRINTING
TIINCNDE	=	INCIDENT
ALUP RMNAIT	=	PAUL MARTIN
WLO EYK	=	LOW KEY

PHOTO TERMS

GHLTNTEISUIO	=	SILHOUETTING
YDBO PCA	=	BODY CAP
EFYSEHI NELS	=	FISHEYE LENS
ACTNRIU	=	CURTAIN
EOKHB	=	BOKEH
ALLB EHAD	=	BALL HEAD
HSLAF LBUB	=	FLASH BULB
NSEL UMTON	=	LENS MOUNT
CDAOKBPR	=	BACKDROP
IBDROUO	=	BOUDOIR
CEBUON DARC	=	BOUNCE CARD
DKKAO	=	KODAK

PHOTO TERMS

TOPSANBROI = ABSORPTION

IADTFCRFINO = DIFFRACTION

SRUAOOCIRHC = CHIAROSCURO

EDFFUIS = DIFFUSE

MRAOHC = CHROMA

USUOFY RASKH = YOUSUF KARSH

LCFOA HLNTGE = FOCAL LENGTH

ANBK HLGTI = BANK LIGHT

RBLEAR = BARREL

LAENS SDAMA = ANSEL ADAMS

HOIMTARCC = CHROMATIC

FTOS SCFUO = SOFT FOCUS

PHOTO TERMS

ADMTAAET	=	METADATA
AYHSIAC	=	YASHICA
FFO AACMRE	=	OFF CAMERA
AEPPR AFES	=	PAPER SAFE
TPAPHGHOYOR	=	PHOTOGRAPHY
EPXIL	=	PIXEL
RAZEPIOLR	=	POLARIZER
SPERSPRE	=	PREPRESS
GRMAPRO	=	PROGRAM
AORDI EAVSL	=	RADIO SLAVE
EYMRYSTM	=	SYMMETRY
YSNC OCRD	=	SYNC CORD

PHOTO TERMS

IUATAORNST	=	SATURATION
UIJF	=	FUJI
REIFB CTPIOS	=	FIBER OPTICS
OSTOH	=	SHOOT
LOFOD AMLP	=	FLOOD LAMP
OTOF ANCLDE	=	FOOT CANDLE
LLUF PTSO	=	FULL STOP
AMETT	=	MATTE
SBHEASDLAL	=	HASSELBLAD
ESCOL OSFCU	=	CLOSE FOCUS
GEG TECAR	=	EGG CRATE
PTGIFOHROL	=	LIGHTPROOF

PHOTO TERMS

NIOKTGNESY	=	KEYSTONING
THETRUS GLA	=	SHUTTER LAG
FAEL HTRSTEU	=	LEAF SHUTTER
ESLN LCCIER	=	LENS CIRCLE
EKRKIC GHTLI	=	KICKER LIGHT
OORLAPID	=	POLAROID
ENLS LBEARR	=	LENS BARREL
ENLS NATGOIC	=	LENS COATING
ITK	=	KIT
AERGL MATOFR	=	LARGE FORMAT
SENL APC	=	LENS CAP
SNLE DOHO	=	LENS HOOD

PHOTO TERMS

F PSOT	=	F STOP
ORFTAM	=	FORMAT
GNOL NLSE	=	LONG LENS
CGAMI UHRO	=	MAGIC HOUR
F BENMRU	=	F NUMBER
EARMF	=	FRAME
LGE	=	GEL
ELEOTFRCR	=	REFLECTOR
MCAFOERO	=	FOAMCORE
IRAFMNG	=	FRAMING
ANEGELTI	=	GELATINE
MICRS	=	SCRIM

PHOTO TERMS

EERMT	=	METER
LIMUSN	=	MUSLIN
YSUOPLM	=	OLYMPUS
AEPTLS	=	PASTEL
OEHGPOTARPHR	=	PHOTOGRAPHER
YNSC ALDYE	=	SYNC DELAY
OMOZ HSALF	=	ZOOM FLASH
VVEARTESPIER	=	PRESERVATIVE
RAPRMGO EA	=	PROGRAM AE
OMZO NI	=	ZOOM IN
CRTLAIRNIEE	=	RECTILINEAR
OEGAETRPR	=	REPORTAGE

PHOTO TERMS

NUME	=	MENU
TEOUMIATCDL	=	MULTICOATED
JOBCTE ELSN	=	OBJECT LENS
DUTIOS SELN	=	STUDIO LENS
NDWWOI ITGHL	=	WINDOW LIGHT
EPHILON	=	PINHOLE
INPOT ORCUSE	=	POINT SOURCE
EPWOR OZMO	=	POWER ZOOM
CSSOPRE ENLS	=	PROCESS LENS
JTSCBEU	=	SUBJECT
EEEDCR	=	RECEDE
BTERADNRM	=	REMBRANDT

PHOTO TERMS

HEOS	=	SHOE
HLITG LTRIA	=	LIGHT TRAIL
SELCUPO	=	CLOSEUP
OIZECOLR	=	COLORIZE
LORCO ACST	=	COLOR CAST
RCOLO HIFST	=	COLOR SHIFT
IEDED DSMAA	=	EDDIE ADAMS
OCFSU	=	FOCUS
EEGWEE	=	WEEGEE
TRETBYA ACKP	=	BATTERY PACK
EGRNE RSECEN	=	GREEN SCREEN
LBRU	=	BLUR

PHOTO TERMS

ONDIGONCRHAL	=	HANDCOLORING
THA CRKIT	=	HAT TRICK
NWETOS	=	WESTON
LOHD KABC	=	HOLD BACK
ESLN ESHAD	=	LENS SHADE
THO AMLP	=	HOT LAMP
EOSH DRAPTEA	=	SHOE ADAPTER
NLELNACIIMU	=	ILLUMINANCE
EMIAG ANLEP	=	IMAGE PLANE
NODORI DEMO	=	INDOOR MODE
FLES IRTEM	=	SELF TIMER
COLOWTT	=	WOLCOTT

PHOTO TERMS

OLRICFIMM	=	MICROFILM
NYCS DPSEE	=	SYNC SPEED
OMZO SELN	=	ZOOM LENS
MOOZ TOU	=	ZOOM OUT
RAET TSHEE	=	TEAR SHEET
CTKA APSRH	=	TACK SHARP
OPP	=	POP
ERTSPE OCSFU	=	PRESET FOCUS
RPAOGMR ODME	=	PROGRAM MODE
KAER GITHL	=	RAKE LIGHT
LERCYCE MEIT	=	RECYCLE TIME
DPEORORNCTIU	=	REPRODUCTION

PHOTO TERMS

OMYMER	=	MEMORY
UMDDY	=	MUDDY
ETJOBC	=	OBJECT
TOCSK OHTOP	=	STOCK PHOTO
OCNOHTPEIG	=	PHOTOGENIC
UDOSIT	=	STUDIO
OPNIT	=	POINT
RPOWE INDWER	=	POWER WINDER
ORPSNSGICE	=	PROCESSING
ITWEH IHLTG	=	WHITE LIGHT
EWID NEOP	=	WIDE OPEN
NDIW NAMHICE	=	WIND MACHINE

PHOTO TERMS

ETCACN HGTLI	=	ACCENT LIGHT
WRA	=	RAW
RLEGERAN	=	ENLARGER
GDIAILT	=	DIGITAL
ECHVRAI	=	ARCHIVE
SYATMMREY	=	ASYMMETRY
WIDEN DNLA	=	EDWIN LAND
AEBRULBB	=	BAREBULB
LCCKI	=	CLICK
LEGAN WEOLLR	=	GALEN ROWELL
VIGTNEEA	=	NEGATIVE
WNLOB UTO	=	BLOWN OUT

PHOTO TERMS

OBNCEU TILHG	=	BOUNCE LIGHT
HGLIT ARTP	=	LIGHT TRAP
OLFLAFF	=	FALLOFF
DIENFR	=	FINDER
SFALH NGU	=	FLASH GUN
OSCFU GNIR	=	FOCUS RING
LFUL ECAF	=	FULL FACE
AEGRL GELAN	=	GLARE ANGLE
LSMI SANORA	=	SLIM AARONS
YRAG DACR	=	GRAY CARD
DIGR	=	GRID
OGURDN SLSGA	=	GROUND GLASS

PHOTO TERMS

LNOTA ENARG	=	TONAL RANGE
IAREAL HOOTP	=	AERIAL PHOTO
RHLDCAOTK	=	DARKCLOTH
TORBRE ACAP	=	ROBERT CAPA
TANI ESAHK	=	ANTI SHAKE
KORMORAD	=	DARKROOM
CNRBEKAIGT	=	BRACKETING
ATXIRM	=	MATRIX
NISTOECAMPNO	=	COMPENSATION
EHCAB EODM	=	BEACH MODE
ORARGPM EMDO	=	PROGRAM MODE
ELE EMLIRL	=	LEE MILLER

PHOTO TERMS

NTCPLPIIOAA	=	APPLICATION
IMIATGSTMAS	=	ASTIGMATISM
GRAHIADPM	=	DIAPHRAGM
AYBB TPOS	=	BABY SPOT
ICLKC OTSP	=	CLICK STOP
SENIONTEX	=	EXTENSION
DBNEL	=	BLEND
SELEA	=	EASEL
LBBU EDOM	=	BULB MODE
IOGZT	=	GITZO
LILF HLITG	=	FILL LIGHT
MRUEELI	=	LUMIERE

1.

Taking pictures is savoring life

intensely, every hundredth of a second.

Marc Riboud

2.

A tear contains an ocean. A photographer

is aware of the tiny moments in a persons

life that reveal greater truths. Anon

3.

A good photograph is one that communicates a

fact, touches the heart and leaves the viewer a

changed person for having seen it. It is,

in a word, effective. Irving Penn

4.

In the world of photography, you get

to share a captured moment with other

people. James Wilson

5.

Once the amateurs naive approach and humble
willingness to learn fades away, the
creative spirit of good photography dies with
it. Alfred Eisenstaedt

6.

Kodak sells film, but they dont advertise
film; they advertise memories. Theodore
Levitt

7.

A photograph is like a recipe the memory is
the finished dish. Carrie Latet

8.

To me, photography is the simultaneous
recognition, in a fraction of a second,
of the significance of an event. Henri
Cartier-Bresson

9.

If your pictures arent good enough, youre not

close enough. Robert Capa

10.

Taking an image, freezing a moment,

reveals how rich reality truly is. Anon

11.

In photography, the smallest thing can be

a great subject. The little, human detail

can become a Leitmotiv. Henri Cartier-Bresson

12.

Photography is an immediate reaction,

drawing is a meditation. Henri

Cartier-Bresson

13.

You dont take pictures; they take you. - Jay
Maisel

14.

Most things in life are moments of pleasure

and a lifetime of embarrassment;

photography is a moment of embarrassment and a

lifetime of pleasure. Tony Benn

15.

Once photography enters your bloodstream, it

is like a disease. Anon

16.

If I could tell the story in words, I

wouldnt need to lug around a camera. Lewis

Hine

17.

Taking pictures is like tiptoeing into the
kitchen late at night and stealing Oreo
cookies. Diane Arbus

18.

When words become unclear, I shall focus
with photographs. When images become
inadequate, I shall be content with silence.
Ansel Adams

19.

Photography deals exquisitely with
appearances, but nothing is what it
appears to be. Duane Michals

20.

In photography there are no shadows that cannot
be illuminated. August Sander

21.

To me, photography is an art of observation.

Its not just about finding something

interesting in an ordinary place Ive

found it has everything to do with the way you

see them. Elliott Erwitt

22.

I think good dreaming is what leads to good

photographs. Wayne Miller

23.

Photography is a major force in explaining

man to man. Edward Steichen

24.

The picture that you took with your camera

is the imagination you want to create with

reality. Scott Lorenzo

25.

There are always two people in every
picture: the photographer and the
viewer. Ansel Adams

26.

A photograph is a secret about a secret. The
more it tells you the less you know. Diane
Arbus

27.

When you photograph a face . . .you
photograph the soul behind it. Jean-Luc
Godard

28.

If you want to be a better photographer,
stand in front of more interesting stuff. Jim
Richardson

29.

My own eyes are no more than scouts on a

preliminary search, the cameras eye may

entirely change my idea. Edward Weston

30.

The camera is an excuse to be someplace you

otherwise dont belong. It gives me both a

point of connection and a point of separation.

Susan Meiselas

31.

Your photography is a record of your living,

for anyone who really sees. Paul Strand

32.

I dont trust words. I trust pictures.

Gilles Peress

33.

You dont take a photograph, you make

it. Ansel Adams

34.

Your first 10,000 photographs are your

worst. Henri Cartier-Bresson

35.

Life is like a camera. Just focus on whats

important and capture the good times, develop

from the negatives and if things dont work

out, just take another shot. Anon

36.

My ultimate goal is to try to make the

ordinary look extraordinary Martin

Parr

37.

Photography is the recording of strangeness and beauty with beguiling precision. Sebastian Smee

38.

Beauty can be seen in all things, seeing and composing the beauty is what separates the snapshot from the photograph. Matt Hardy

39.

The camera sees more than the eye, so why not make use of it? Edward Weston

40.

There is one thing the photograph must contain the humanity of the moment. Robert Frank

41.

One doesnt stop seeing. One doesnt stop

framing. It doesnt turn off and turn on. Its on

all the time. Annie Leibovitz

42.

My life is shaped by the urgent need to wander

and observe, and my camera is my passport.

Steve McCurry

43.

When I photograph, what Im really doing is

seeking answers to things. Wynn Bullock

44.

We are making photographs to

understand what our lives mean to us.

Ralph Hattersley

45.

A portrait is not made in the camera but on

either side of it. Edward Steichen

46.

The camera is an instrument that

teaches people how to see without a camera.

Dorothea Lange

47.

Its one thing to make a picture of what a

person looks like, its another thing to make a

portrait of who they are. Paul Caponigro

48.

With photography a new language has been

created. We can look at an impression as long

as we wish, we can delve into it and, so

to speak, renew past experiences at will. -

Anon

49.

My idea of a good picture is one thats

in focus and of a famous person. Andy

Warhol

50.

What I like about photographs is that

they capture a moment thats gone forever,

impossible to reproduce. Karl

Lagerfeld

51.

Photography is a means by which we learn to

see the ordinary. David Bailey

52.

Actually, Im not all that interested in the

subject of photography. Once the picture is in

the box, Im not all that interested in what

happens next. Hunters, after all, arent cooks.

Henri Cartier-Bresson

53.

When people ask me what equipment I use I

tell them my eyes. Anon

54.

Look and think before opening the shutter.

The heart and mind are the true lens of the

camera. Yousuf Karsh

55.

Life is too short to see someone you love in

bad lighting - Anon

56.

Great photography is about depth of

feeling, not depth of field. Peter Adams

57.

It is more important to click with people than
to click the shutter. Alfred Eisenstaedt

58.

The whole point of taking pictures is so
that you dont have to explain things with
words. Elliott Erwitt

59.

If you see something that moves you, and
then snap it, you keep a moment. Linda
McCartney

60.

I wish that all of natures magnificence,
the emotion of the land, the living energy
of place could be photographed. Annie
Leibovitz

61.

Photograph: a picture painted by the sun

without instruction in art. Ambrose Bierce

62.

Photography is the story I fail to put into

words. Destin Sparks

63.

I love the people I photograph. I mean,

theyre my friends. Ive never met most of them

or I dont know them at all, yet through my

images I live with them. Bruce Gilden

64.

Once you learn to care, you can record images

with your mind or on film. There is no

difference between the two. Anon

65.

I really believe there are things nobody
would see if I didnt photograph them. Diane
Arbus

66.

Photography has no rules, it is not a
sport. It is the result which counts, no matter
how it is achieved. Bill Brandt

67.

You dont take a photograph. You ask
quietly to borrow it. Anon

68.

Photography is truth. The cinema is truth
twenty-four times per second. Jean-Luc
Godard

69.

I never have taken a picture Ive intended.

Theyre always better or worse. Diane Arbus

70.

The negative is the equivalent of the

composers score and the print, the performance.

 Ansel Adams

71.

The camera makes you forget youre there.

Its not like you are hiding but you forget,

you are just looking so much. Annie Leibovitz

72.

Essentially what photography is is life

lit up. Sam Abell

73.

The best thing about a picture is that it never changes, even when the people in it do. Andy Warhol

74.

Photography is an austere and blazing poetry of the real. Ansel Adams

75.

If the photographer is interested in the people in front of his lens, and if he is compassionate, its already a lot. The instrument is not the camera but the photographer. Eve Arnold

76.

All photographs are accurate. None of them is the truth. Richard Avedon

77.

A thing that you see in my pictures is that I

was not afraid to fall in love with these

people. Annie Leibovitz

78.

In photography, there is a reality so subtle

that it becomes more real than reality.

Alfred Stieglitz

79.

Photography takes an instant out of time,

altering life by holding it still.

Dorothea Lange

80.

Only photograph what you love. Tim Walker

Want Even MORE Themed Puzzle fun?
Try These!

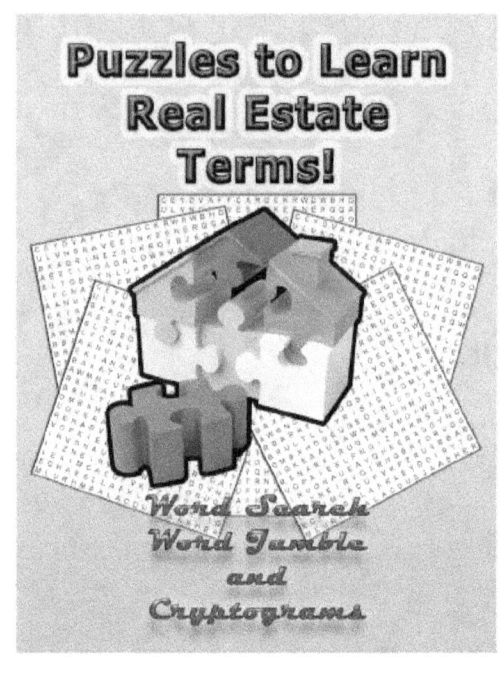

Puzzles To Learn Real Estate Terms!
https://www.amazon.com/dp/1079170758

Music Themed Puzzles
https://www.amazon.com/dp/B07Y4LM6NZ

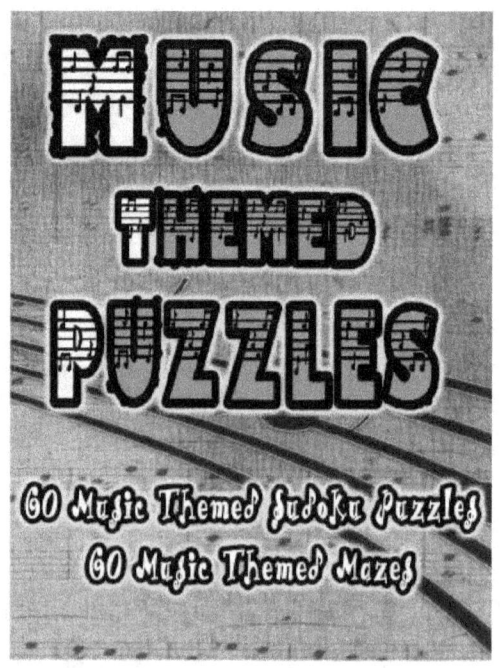

Want Even MORE Themed Puzzle fun?
Try These!

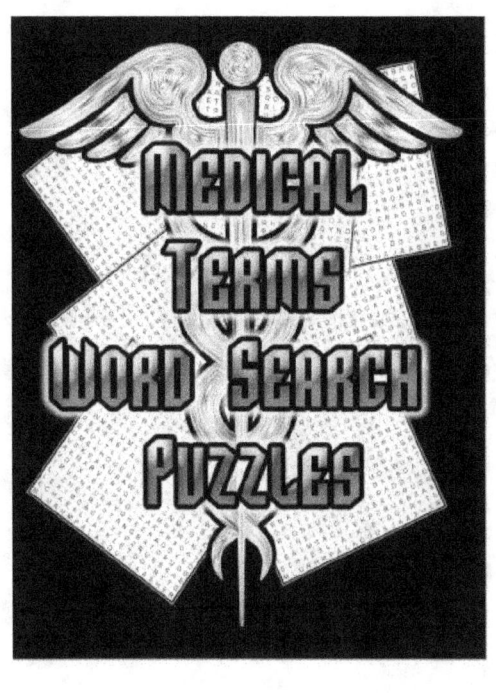

Medical Terms Word Search Puzzles
https://www.amazon.com/dp/1070711772

140 Photography Puzzles
https://www.amazon.com/dp/1070835072

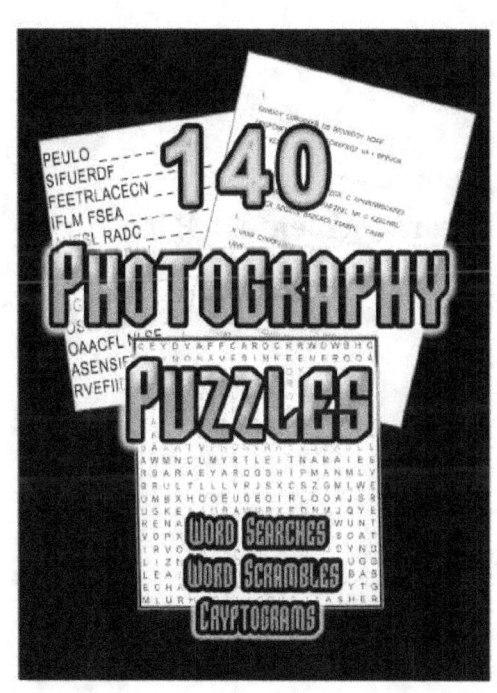

Want Even MORE Themed Puzzle fun?
Try These!

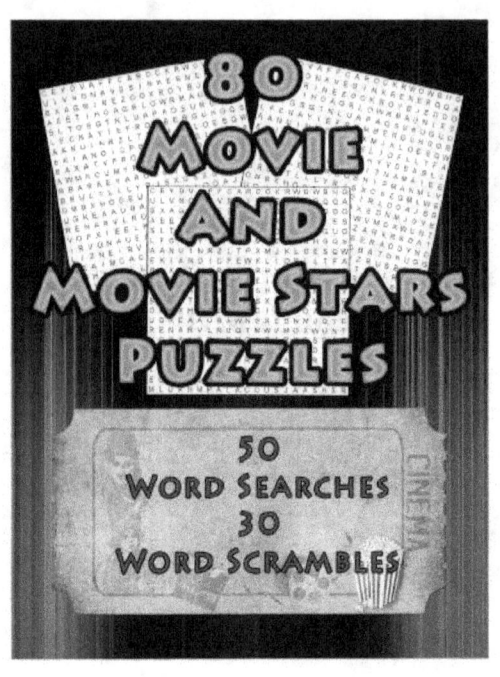

80 Movie And Movie Stars Puzzles
https://www.amazon.com/dp/1071448099

Music's Greatest Hits
100 Word Search Puzzles
https://www.amazon.com/dp/107233397X

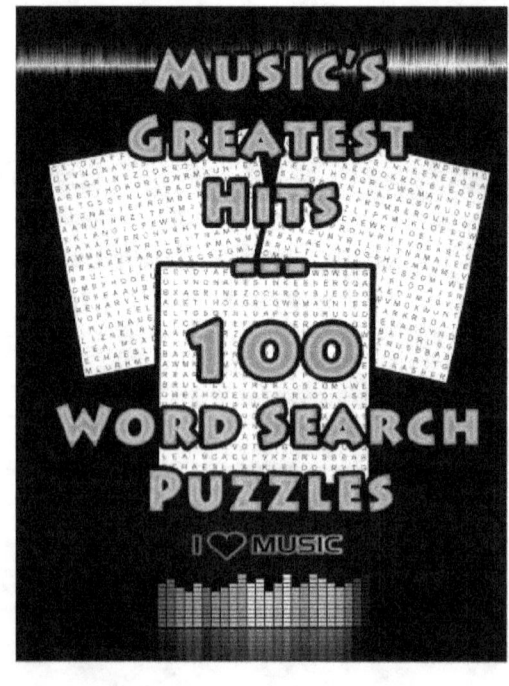

Want Even MORE Themed Puzzle fun?
Try These!

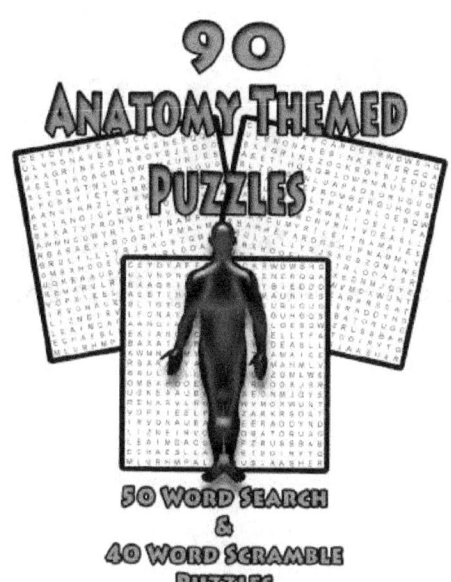

90 Anatomy Themed Puzzles
https://www.amazon.com/dp/1072719177

300 LOL Cryptograms
https://www.amazon.com/dp/107597934X

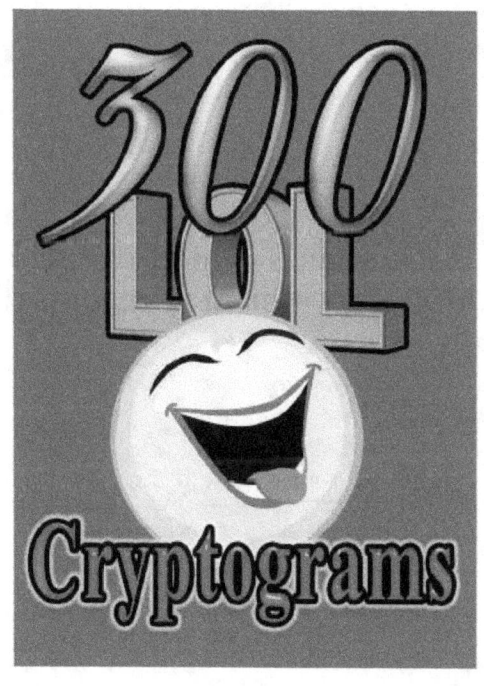

Want Even MORE Puzzle fun?
Try These Holiday Themed Puzzles!

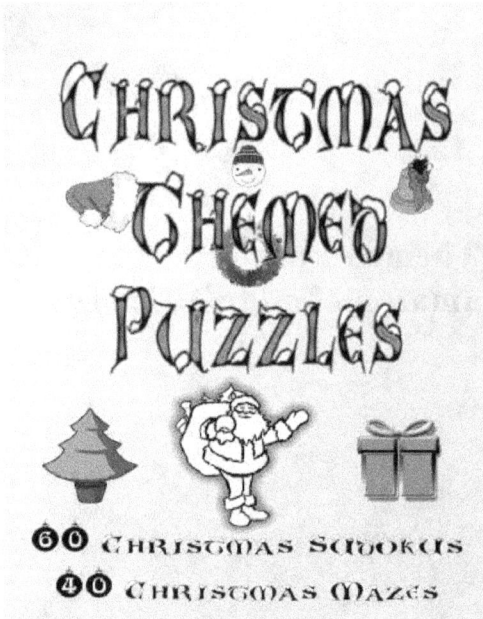

Christmas Themed Puzzles
https://www.amazon.com/dp/1693275082

Halloween Themed Puzzles
https://www.amazon.com/dp/169285724X

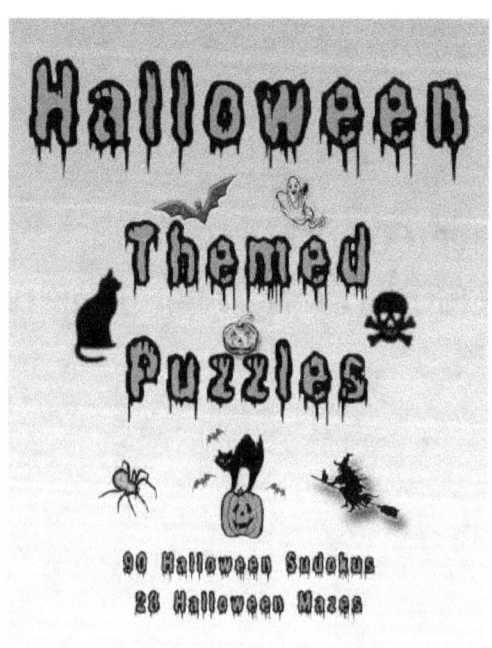

Want Even MORE Puzzle fun?
Try These Holiday Themed Puzzles!

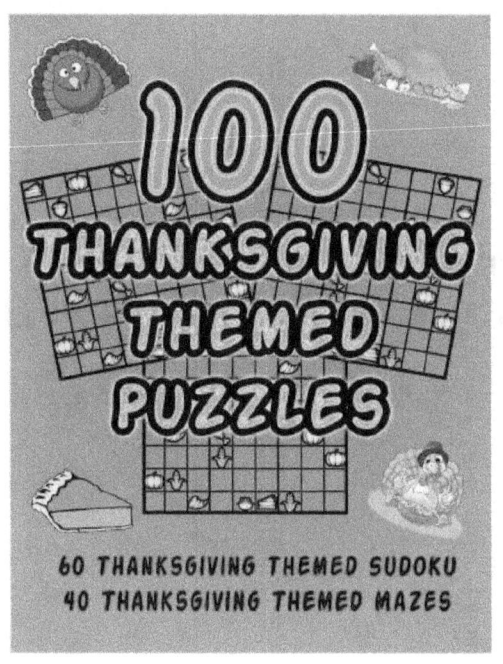

Thanksgiving Themed Puzzles
https://www.amazon.com/dp/1695000056

New Year Themed Puzzlcs
https://www.amazon.com/dp/169568043X

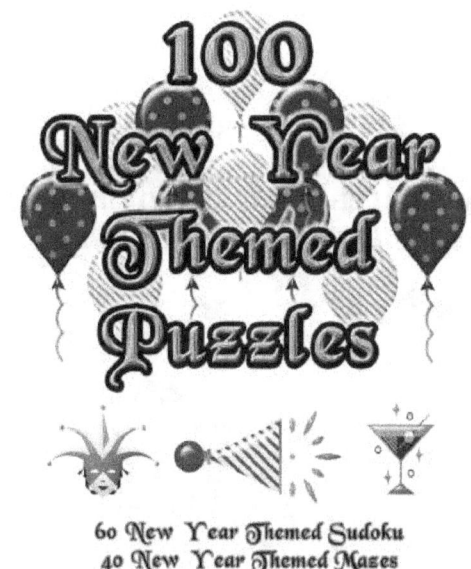

Want Even MORE Puzzle fun?
Try These Holiday Themed Puzzles!

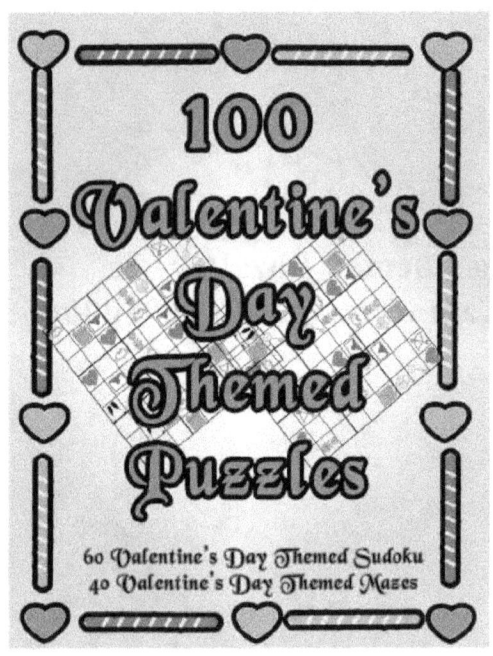

Valentine's Day Themed Puzzles
https://www.amazon.com/dp/1696425603

St. Patrick's Day Themed Puzzles
https://www.amazon.com/dp/1697214150

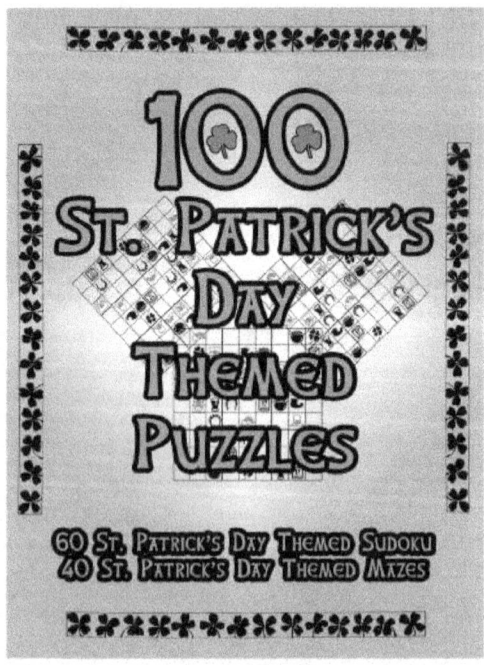

Want Even MORE Puzzle fun?
Try These Holiday Themed Puzzles!

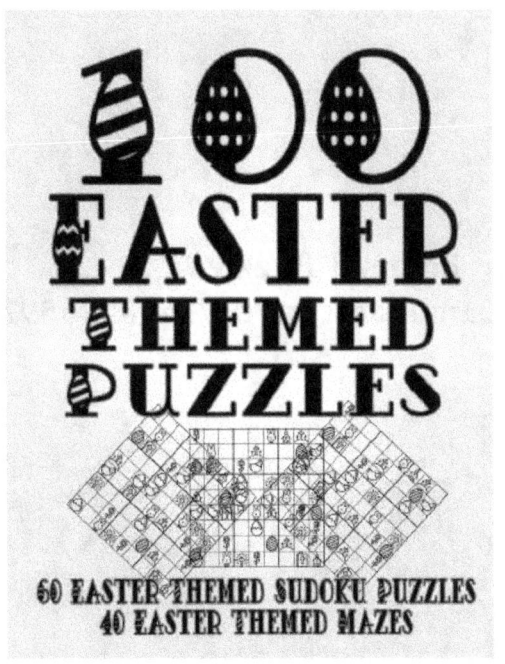

Easter Themed Puzzles
https://www.amazon.com/dp/1697875556

Mother's Day Themed Puzzles
https://www.amazon.com/dp/1698375387

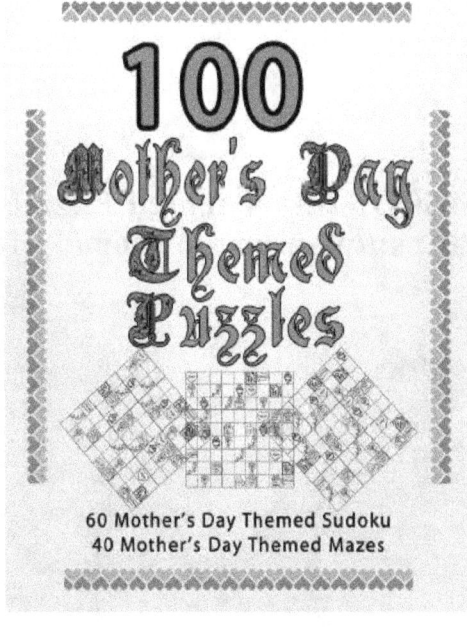

Want Even MORE Puzzle fun?
Try These Holiday Themed Puzzles!

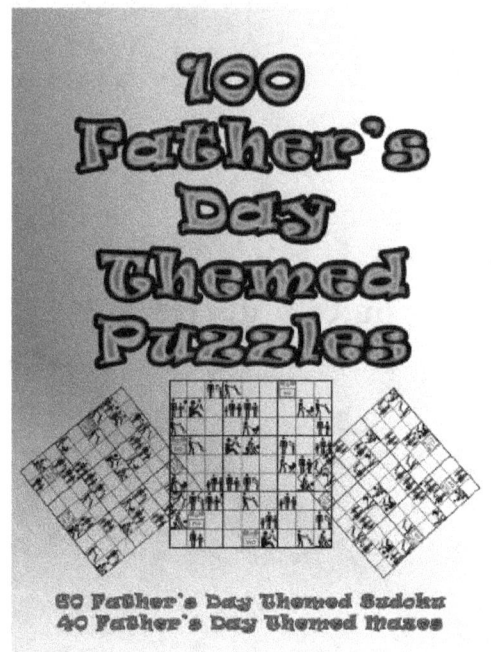

Father's Day Themed Puzzles
https://www.amazon.com/dp/1698823592

4th Of July Themed Puzzles
https://www.amazon.com/dp/169928539X

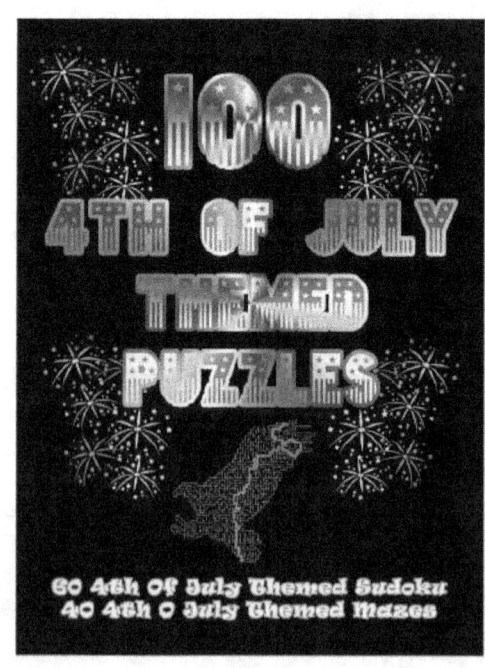